Machiavellian Economics

Second, revised edition

by

Alan F. Bartlett

Second, revised edition published by
Ashford Press Publishing 1987,
1 Church Road,
Shedfield,
Hampshire SO3 2HW.

First published by Schumacher Ltd, England and Switzerland, 1986.

British Library Cataloguing in Publication Data

Bartlett, Alan F.
  Machiavellian economics. – 2nd rev. ed.
  1. Managerial economics
  I. Title
  330'.024658 HD30.22

  ISBN 1-85253-039-1

Typeset by Graphic Image, Cosham
Printed by Robert Hartnoll (1985) Ltd., Bodmin, Cornwall

Contents

Machiavellian Economics

A Book

- to be read, digested and challenged, but not ignored.

- to be hated by politicians who survive through division and rule through discord.

- that equates economics with the activity of man regardless of religion and current morality.

- that promotes economic warfare but spurns nuclear deterrents as weapons of national political blackmail.

- that defines a spade as a digging implement and avoids the popular connotation of a shovel.

Previous publications by the same author.

Profile of the Entrepreneur
Power, Prejudice and Pride
The Banyan Tree

Dedicated to all those who have knowingly and unknowingly helped me along a most exciting path, my family, friends and colleagues, past and present and all too numerous to mention without the risk of omission.

Introduction

Machiavelli is often maligned but seldom misunderstood. He was an impartial observer of princes and people. Fortunately for the author and the reader, people in the mass never change. We have only to substitute politicians for princes and Machiavelli lives on.

The master observed that the driving force of princes was their constant pursuit of power. He noted the inevitable repetition of patterns of behaviour brought about by the consistent ambition of the few to dominate the many and that success in domination was equated to power.

Power is exerted over people. It exists when people either do as they are told or refrain from doing that which they would otherwise have done. Above all, power can never be taken, it is always given. The transfer of power is an act of abdication and not, as fondly imagined, one of delegation. Transfer is absolute.

At first sight it is difficult to understand why, with these limitations and their implications, power should be freely offered. The answer lies in the fallibility of human confidence.

Those who desire power first seek to generate one or more of the three basic human emotions of fear, envy and greed in the minds of those they wish to dominate. This is achieved by presenting a problem or an opportunity whose resolution or satisfaction will benefit those whose emotions are to be aroused. The clinching factor is the offer by the presenter to assume the responsibility for ensuring a successful conclusion. "Do as I say and you will have nothing to fear." "Let me be your leader and you will be as rich, if not richer, than your neighbours." "Follow me and we will destroy those who seek to destroy us." The words have a familiar ring throughout the ages of man. Those who offer their power in return for leadership by others become dependent upon those who accept their offer. Thereafter they are emasculated.

The transfer is not only made freely, it is often a matter for rejoicing. People have been relieved of the burden of responsibility. Whether subsequently the benefit of relief is far outweighed by new burdens is by then irrelevant. The acceptor is well beyond the control or influence of those who have made him their proxy. Since power is given and never taken, its recovery is not a simple matter of reversing to regain the original position. Those who afterwards regret their original offer find that it cannot be withdrawn by unilateral decision. The contract is binding and both parties have to agree to its later cancellation or amendment. History has shown that the practical resolution of the problem created by abdication is the death of the overt wielder of the power.

Those who have decided to use cautiously and jealously the power given to them have been able to pass some, if not all of it, on to succeeding generations. Where the inheritors of power have applied the same constraints and restraints, they also have been able to forge new links in a chain of continuity. Examples are to be found in religion, education and western aristocracy. Pockets of power have survived, albeit some with periods of complete obscurity and apparent absence. They continue to influence and sometimes control huge masses of people who are ignorant successors to forebears who originally handed over their birthright. The passage of time has been so long and the original incident so unremarked that such ignorance is no surprise.

Eruptions of discrete power occur where economic and political developments uncover opportunities that encourage mass response to the baits of fear, greed and envy. There have been many examples of relatively short lived overt power. Dictators have been created and destroyed. Royal houses have been built and pulled down. Empires have spread far and wide but still have faded away into oblivion.

Machiavellian Economics is concerned with these eruptions of power. They are the violent and often self-destructive machinations that determine the physical comfort and welfare of nations. They are the cause of war, revolution and physical disruption. They are governed by the laws of human behaviour that have no connection with the cornerstones of continuity power. Eruptions of power invoke faith and trust solely as weapons of propaganda, but accept neither.

That is not to say that Machiavellian Economics is more devious or less morally attractive than the study of the continuity of power. Short-term eruptions and centuries of continuity of power are two sides of the same coin — Man. Both reflect the foibles, frailties and strengths of human beings. To compare one side with the other in terms of good and bad is a waste of time and effort. Man is what he is. That which he might be, is a subject for the philosopher. That which he is, is the study of the economist.

There are those who pontificate as to what man "should" or "should not do". They speak perpetually in the conditional and set targets, yardsticks and goals. They are usually teachers of philosophy or religion, who have a valuable contribution to make to the evolution of man in his quest for improvement, since without them man would be a one-sided coin, or even a double-headed disc. In either guise, he would be of little value except for slot machines and gambling so that his prosperity would only last as long as his duplicity remained undiscovered.

Machiavellian Economics accepts that there are two sides to the character of man and recognises the existence of the conditional morality, but it concentrates on its study on what can be forecast and ignores that which is based on faith or trust and depends upon the unquantifiable strength of feelings and personal motivation. Man can be assisted in his pursuance of material gain by guidance related to the future which in turn can only be derived from what has actually happened. Machiavellian Economics attempts its task on the premise that man in the mass follows a pre-determinable pattern of behaviour in the pursuit of his material gain and his self preservation, knowledge which has been identified and used by princes over the course of many centuries of civilisation. Today it is manipulated in the main by politicians who, because of the absence of the aura attributed to those born to lead, have been forced to create an interrelationship with those they seek to command. Thus the development of democracy. This has become an inextricable and essential part of the symmetry of economics. In the past the feudal system was easily understood and applied. The modern concept of democracy is extremely complex as it seeks to manipulate the majority into an acceptance of rule by the minority. In so doing, the mass of the populace becomes a tangled knotted bundle with those who seek to govern caught up in their own web of prevarication and vote-seeking promises. Inevitably the only solution to periodic rationalisation is a sharp knife — effective but painful.

The pursuit of power is the economics of man. Those who seek power become the catalysts and those who give it establish the behaviour pattern. The seekers need authority and resources. Authority is provided by people. Its continuance depends upon the support of resources.

The study of Economics is not confined to the behaviour of man, whether he seeks or abdicates power. It also involves the examination of resources available to him and their alternative uses.

Power is an end in itself. Those who seek it do not need justification. Their satisfaction arises from the reaction of those who recognise the authority and fear of its existence. The threat is many times more potent than the use.

The first objective of Machiavellian Economics is to study without bias or prejudice the probable future environment within which man will have to survive and hopefully prosper. That necessitates a number of commercial and technological assumptions which can only be tested in theory.

The second task is to identify the behaviour patterns of the past and relate them to the relevant past environments, ignoring the temptation of assuming motivation. It will be found that even the inconsistency of men is constant, given repetitive situations.

The two sets of data are then examined in relation one to the other with particular reference to possible inter-reaction, in order to produce finally the optimum probability of repetition in known circumstances. At that point, other assumptions relating to political and philosophical intervention can be built into the model, again with the hindsight of probable reaction and effect.

The main hurdle in establishing any specific economic policy is the conflict between those who seek power who will attempt to intervene competitively and might well depend upon misrepresentation to achieve their aims. It is quite unlikely that that impediment will ever disappear whilst man remains as he is. If the principles hereinafter presented are accepted and applied, the least benefit that will be derived from their application will be a better understanding of the alternatives open to man and the implications of choice. He might even be able to resist the promises of those who seek their own promotion in the offer of his.

Machiavelli 1515 and Economics 1986

Machiavelli was an observer and an analyst. His observations led him towards certain conclusions which have withstood the test of time.

Since economics is the study of the behaviour of man and that pattern has not changed since the times of Machiavelli, then it would seem reasonable that his conclusions are equally valid today. If that is so, then they can provide the guidelines which modern man desperately needs to forecast the probable outcome of his present decisions or indecisiveness.

Examples of some of Machiavelli's conclusions are given hereunder. They need little explanation.

The Challenge and Response to Challenge

"There is nothing more difficult to carry out, nor more doubtful of success, nor more dangerous to handle, than to initiate a new order of things. For the reformer has enemies in all those who profit by the old order of things and only luke-warm defenders in all those who would profit by the new order, this lukewarmness arising partly from fear of the adversaries and partly from the incredulity of mankind, who do not truly believe in anything new until they have had practical experience of it."

The human reaction to change is well understood by politicians who will seldom undertake the responsibility for its implementation, knowing full well the antagonism as well as the opportunity given to political opponents.

People are fearful of change. By its very definition it introduces the unknown. However dirty or squalid conditions may appear to the onlooker, those living in them will resist improvement. The more radical the imposed change, the greater the resistance.

An obvious example of this has been in the planning and

implementation of urban development. Row upon row of insanitary cottages built originally by profit motivated instructors or similarly motivated employers are condemned by all and sundry as unfit for human habitation. And yet the offer of space and hygiene in the shape of a modern featureless high rise block of flats is rejected by those who would appear to gain the most, the tenants of the cramped unwholesome terraces. It is the contrast that deters, but it is the exchange of the known for the unknown that leads to the blank refusal. The pendulum has swung too far and the transitional gap is too wide.

Individuals will always retreat into the safety of their accustomed surroundings. For that purpose, the smaller and more cramped that they are, the more loath are the inhabitants to leave. The conditions may not be comfortable, but at least in their certainty they are comforting.

Change is like success. Those who promote it risk a great deal. Those who succeed in its implementation are likely to be thrust aside in the rush for recognition. Successful change has many authors for the simple reason that it is rare and even then the outcome of inevitability.

Judged by Results

"How dangerous it is to take the lead in a new enterprise in which many may be concerned and how difficult it is to handle and direct it and once directed on its way to keep it going. For men judge an action by the result."

Once again, the politician has no desire to make himself vulnerable. To sell a concept is relatively easy. To translate it into profit takes an inordinant amount of time and effort.

Economic performance is a treadmill. The entrepreneur will encourage expectations to obtain support in his early endeavours. If he progresses, then his results confirm his promises and from there on the momentum is often beyond his control and direction. His targets are set by the expectations of others which they will extrapolate. His rate of growth is determined for him and it requires an entrepreneur of unusual strength of character to deny himself publicly. It is far easier for him to embrace the hopes of others, bask in their premature congratulations and accept their gratitude for their anticipated income to be derived from his future achievements.

The Attraction of Doing Nothing

"But the worse thing about weak republics is that they are irresolute so that all the choices they make, they are forced to make; and, if they should happen to do the right thing, it is force, not their own good sense that makes them do it, for their weakness does not allow them to arrive at a decision where there is any doubt; and unless this doubt is removed by some compelling act of violence, they remain ever in suspense."

Decision making is the act of choice. When there is no alternative and a particular decision is unavoidable, then it is no longer a positive action and the outcome is entirely left to chance. It is very difficult to identify responsibility for inactivity. Thus the bank manager who does not grant a loan cannot leave himself open to criticism thereafter in the event that the borrower is unable to repay. The fact that the intended borrower succeeds through the help of another bank is not regarded as criticism of the first who failed to support the would-be entrepreneur. There are many reasons that can be concocted subsequent to success to justify the refusal. The career of many men is dependent more on their omission of mistakes than on their commission of success.

Weakness is a self-perpetuating characteristic. There are times when glorious inactivity is right, but even then it must be the outcome of a conscious evaluation of the options that are available. It may be necessary to pause in the long climb to recover and regroup. Batteries may need recharging or a fresh look taken at the terrain ahead. The pause can only be momentary, deliberately selected and used. Deliberation may be the antecedent to action but progress can only be the outcome of action.

Ignoring the Experience of Others

"If one examines with diligence the past, it is easy to foresee the future of any commonwealth and to apply those remedies that were used of old: or, if one does not find that remedy was used, to devise new ones owing to the similarity between events. But, since such studies are neglected and what is read is not understood, or if it is understood is not applied in practice by those who rule, the consequence is that similar troubles occur at all times."

History is inevitably assessed from one particular point of view. Consequently the conclusions drawn from its examination are biased and misleading. They are further confused by national pride, fear of the unacceptable and rejection.

It is often the fact that an objective analysis of some past event or conditions will offer an extremely uncomfortable parallel with a similar current situation, so that it may be distorted or even suppressed. Since the beginning of the Industrial Revolution, the United Kingdom has repeated very many identical economic/political mistakes that have been tolerated only through absolute ignorance of the factors that actually lay behind the original errors.

Doing the Right Thing at the Right Time

"In what they do some men are impetuous, others look about them and are cautious. Since they go to extremes and are unable to go about things in the right way, in both cases they make mistakes. On the other hand, he is likely to make fewer mistakes and to prosper in his fortune when circumstances accord with his conduct and one always proceeds as the force of nature compels one."

Strategy is the art of doing the right thing at the right time. What is correct today is not necessarily so tomorrow.

To be at the right place at the right time may necessitate sailing against the wind. Sailing downwind is an attractive proposition but it is in the opposite direction that the yachtsman makes the most dramatic and direct progress. The successful strategist understands his environment and the effect of the forces that are contained in it.

There is little doubt but that economic environmental changes occur more rapidly as society develops. Products enjoy shorter life cycles and technological innovation in one field often has an unexpected and dramatic effect upon another. It follows that decisions today have to be taken more rapidly than those of yesterday.

Competition grows more fierce as communication is improved. Facts are available to a greater audience more quickly and accurately than ever before. Today, exceptional profit is determined by the speed off the blocks as the time span of the race is being constantly reduced. As the ability of the athlete improves, the middle distance race becomes the sustained sprint.

There is, however, another dimension to the sequence of effort. As the time spent in the market place is more condensed, investment in preparation increases. Technology demands substantial capital investment. Research, exploration and pre-planning take on the role of initiative decisions. These activities also take time. It is therefore reasonable to assume that this new layer of decision-making will dominate the strategy considerations of the future and attract the attention and involvement of the economist. There will also be a greater political element in these problems of choice since the significance and consequences of their resolution will affect many aspects of human life and living. It would appear that the day is not far distant when the economist and politician will have to merge as one. It would be too much to expect a consensus should they remain apart.

Perseverance

"History as a whole bears witness that men may second their fortune, but they cannot oppose it: that they may weave its warp, but cannot break it. Yet, they should never give up, because there is always hope though they know not the end and move towards it along roads which cross one another and as yet are unexplored: and since there is hope they should not despair, no matter what fortune brings or in what travail they find themselves."

There is an awful inevitability in the progress of man. Hidden in his success are the seeds of his failure. Life is fortunately a switchback. Whilst that which goes up must come down, there is also the certainty that having reached the nadir, the next phase is returning upwards.

The above conclusions provide us with a summary of the pattern of behaviour of man. They give us very little guidance as to Machiavelli's conclusions concerning sources of power, but as expressed elsewhere, no matter how astute or competent the man, in the long term he can achieve very little without economic resources.

Power and Behaviour

Sources of Power

Economic power depends upon economic resources. Those who wish to wield power must not only obtain the acquiescence of those who are prepared to abdicate from decision and influence, but also extract the promise from those who own or control economic resources that they will be made available as and when necessary on request.

Those who desire to exercise power ideally prefer to choose that resource which should offer them the most advantage in the pursuit of their objective, but more often than not their choice is thrust upon them by their circumstances or the environment within which they seek to achieve their aims.

Resources are only valuable when limited in supply and consistently in demand. There have been, and remain, only two resources that fall within that definition, namely land and people. They also happen to be in direct contrast, one with the other, in almost all of their attributes except those of measurement of wealth. The demarcation between these two resources has been increased to great effect by the power hungry and has become synonymous with the deep and wide chasm between the haves and havenots, the right and the left, the privileged and the oppressed.

At first sight, land and people resources are nicely balanced. In the short or medium term either provides sufficient support necessary to achieve the most ambitious political ends. But it is a deceptive illusion. Whilst people present a potentially terrifying force that unleashed and directed can wreak havoc in bloody and effective revolution, they are notoriously fickle. They can quickly become disillusioned with or without justification. They can be diverted and misled. In the long term, the scales are grossly out of

11

balance. Economics, unlike Justice, is by no means blind. Reality rules. Consequently power based upon ownership of land must ultimately win the day.

Machiavellian Aspects of Land

Ownership of Land has long been recognised as the cornerstone of economic power and has therefore been most jealously guarded. Since power diminishes according to use, security inherent in Land will seldom be made available even as collateral unless its owners have been persuaded that there is a very real threat to the continuity of their ownership and that the risk entailed in providing security is justified. That not to do so would be to take a far greater risk. The persuaders have demonstrated to the owners' satisfaction that without the promise of the collateral they will be powerless to stop their opponents from stealing some if not all of that most valuable resource. Those who own will naturally support those who proclaim the advantages of private ownership and resist the advances of those who propagate public ownership. Whether either argument benefits society as a whole is irrelevant. It is a most convenient battle-cry, and an equally effective rallying call. The essence of persuasion is selfishness which is politically presented as selflessness. Even when the objective is government by the minority it is assumed to be in the interests of all since the majority must benefit from the strength and competence of the minority who are the only ones capable of leading.

Land has certain attributes that condition its owners to their advantage. It is a solid, quiet, certain and scarce resource. It can be cultivated or left fallow. Climatic conditions may vary but there is an overall inevitable pattern of seasons. Patience must ultimately be rewarded. Land is capable of generating wealth in many ways, some of which may not be identified for centuries. It can sleep undisturbed during the most violent storms. It can erupt and disgorge destruction. It needs little maintenance and can afford to wait. It encourages patience and the use of shadows. It inspires quiet confidence. It is substantial enough to discourage trespass and encroachment. It has created a formidable defence through the laws of custom, usage and statute. Its abuse can be savagely penalised. To inherit Land is to inherit its characteristics, the dominant themes being continuity and avoidance of reduction or loss.

The objectives of landowners have remained constant regardless of generation and circumstances. They can be summarised as:

1. The maintenance of absolute long-term control.

2. The acceptance of short-term eruptions and disturbances where they are unavoidable and do not create a real threat, precedent or obligation.

3. A preference towards anonymity and avoidance of overt expressions of power, wealth and substance — almost a facade of abstract apology.

4. The use of institutions and tradition patiently created in preference to individuals, groups or communities.

5. A constant alertness in identifying dangers and competing interests represented by other sources of land or people that might be capable of providing power bases.

The principle employed is to retain the dominant economic resource at almost any short-term cost and only to expose its strength as a last resort, i.e. when there is an otherwise unavoidable loss of control. It follows therefore that those who are not owners but seek the solid support of land must first persuade its guardians that such a danger truly exists. Hence in the past the constant threat of war and in the present that of social revolution.

Machiavellian Aspects of People

At first sight, People hardly constitute an economic resource and do not compare with Land as a source of potential wealth. The true difference in economic terms is not one of absolute strength and effectiveness but of sustainment and continuity. In the short term, the support of the mass of people can be sufficient to overwhelm those supported by Land. Politicians who enjoy the active contribution of the vast majority of people can direct and instruct those who represent the owners of the Land. The weaknesses of people as human beings limit their effectiveness as an economic resource. Unlike Land they have no latent strength. Their power has to be applied and once the threat has disappeared, they become exposed to counter attack. The standard tactic employed is one of division and that is easily achieved. The first targets are the political leaders who are, if nothing else, pragmatic. They above all others are fully aware of the temporary nature of their term of office. It may well be that their allegiance in the first instance to that particular economic resource was on of expedience. Alternatively, they might have recognised that the quickest route to membership of the establishment was by way of leading a successful revolution. Finally, and most cynically, the promise of inevitable ingratitude offers less inducement than that of comfortable retirement. Politicians who seek the approbation of People in the mass in order to achieve their personal ambitions when the support of Land is not open to them do so in the knowledge that such support is invaluable in the attainment of high office but quite unreliable in its retention. This pattern of political behaviour is predetermined and often repeated.

Similarly, the politician who seeks mass support must concentrate the burden of his message on human rights, the oppression of any minority, the inequality of opportunity, the lack of morality, the imposition of privilege, the inequity of inheritance and the importance of religious principles together with the over-riding significance of the individual — the culminating message for each listener. Fear, greed and envy are the essential planks of his platform. Tradition, inheritance and privilege are the objects of his hatred.

A nation has two resources each of which represents a potential support for those who seek power within that nation. There are cycles of activity wherein those who represent the resource of People will dominate the decision making structures. These cycles are usually quite short lived. The underlying stream of decisions is generated on behalf of those who control the stable wealth of a nation, Land. The consistency and selfishness of the interests in Land more accurately reflect the needs and potential of a nation than the fickle desires and easily influenced reactions of the mass of People that live within its boundaries. Whether such a conclusion is desirable is beyond the orbit of Machiavellian Economics.

The contribution of the politician is that of the busy bee which pollinates more by accident than design the economy in which he or she happens to live. His or her pattern of behaviour is as predeterminable as that of the insect, including ritual dances, posturing and endless noise. The politician also has his sting. Like his counterpart in nature, the length of his career is determined by his ability to avoid its use.

The Machiavellian Aspects of Democracy

Democracy has been defined as government of the people, by the people, for the people. It is seen as the will of the majority restrained by its humanity towards the minority. It is also held out by the so-called developed countries as the most acceptable form of government. The latter description is the only one near the truth and then only if qualified to the extent that democracy is most acceptable to those who enjoy the privilege of governing.

Democracy is the means whereby the few can direct the many. It is the structure of control through pyramidal organisation. By creating layers of command within a society it is practicable for a marginal majority to assume a dictatorial role culminating in a miniscule proportion of the electorate determining without effective opposition the future of a nation. The very principles of democracy ensure that their application creates a means of dictatorship.

The apex of a pyramid is that which catches the eye and the attention. It appears to be the focal point of strength from which emanates the ultimate control of the whole. In fact the true strength of the pyramid is derived from the symmetry of its structure and not from any specific layer. From its base, upwards, each layer is consistently and uniformly smaller than that upon which it depends. The lower layer is larger than that which it supports. Thus in the pyramid of political power, the key to its control is the very shape and substance of the organisation whereby each layer has the ability to determine the constitution of its immediate superior and that such power is one of a simple majority. By starting at the base and sustaining the repetition of that principle consistently upwards through the structure, it is possible to ensure that the whole pyramid will be under the control of a miniscule proportion of the pyramid's population. As long as the chain holds with each link representing 50.01% of the active strength of each layer, democracy is synonymous with dictatorship.

Such a simple and effective system can, and will be, abused. It will be argued in its defence that so far man has been unable to propose a better alternative. It will also be argued that the most effective economic government is that by dictatorship, whether it be labelled fascist, democratic or communist. But these debates are well beyond the confines of Machiavellian Economics. The above description of political organisation is that which is, regardless of whether it is good or bad, abused or not. Its relevance is that it is the means whereby decisions affecting the economic activity of a society are first determined and then implemented. That which it is supposed to represent is irrelevant. It does, however, explain why more often than not the ultimate results of statutes designed to achieve economic objectives are disastrous.

Democracy is one of the significant political structures designed and used by those who seek economic power through the manipulation of people. It is ideally suited to that purpose needing only an insignificant balance of power at its base. It also has the advantage of appearing to be that which it is not, capable of representation and misrepresentation. But above all it diverts the concentration of the inquisitive away from the secret of its control, that is in fact in an upwards direction, towards the stone of its apex from which issue the commands to the faithful.

Politicians have one desire in common. Like the priests of old, they cannot afford to release the secrets of their trade. Whatever the disagreements between religious sects or communities, their leaders will be united in one effort, that is to maintain their followers' ignorance of the truth behind the illusions they cynically practise.

Despite their protestations to the contrary, democracy and Land ownership are incompatible. Land is the base for feudal government. Whilst the superficial structure of the feudal system can be presented as a pyramid, its power is actually based on perimeter control. The population is contained within a boundary. Not surprisingly the system adopts and adapts the characteristics of its basic resource. It seeks to provide all the necessities for living in return for hard work and loyalty. The latter contributions dissuade wishful thinking and looking over fences towards other territories or structures. Living within a boundary with relatively few responsibilities encourages compliance and complacency. It also discourages initiative and change. Ironically, communism as currently practised is as near to the feudal system as is practicable without the continuity of power through inheritance.

Democracy as a control structure lends itself admirably to the management of People based upon their careless acquiescence. The perimeter or feudal control structure is best suited to those who depend upon the ownership of Land as their resource of power.

Patterns of Behaviour

The essential features of human economic behaviour are:

1. It is consistent and predictably repetitive.
2. It is perpetually seeking balance in theory but depends upon imbalance to achieve its results.
3. Motivation is unimportant.
4. Statistics are irrelevant and unreliable.
5. Its primary reaction is against the unknown.
6. It is inter-active and inter-related.

Economic behaviour is predictable because the actions and reactions of human beings are governed by the environment in which they live and work. Past behaviour patterns provide invaluable guides to the future provided that the economist has an accurate and objective assessment of past environments and an analysis of the factors that created them. Given the same circumstances and pressures, people in the mass will react in different ways upon their repetition. The key to successful forecasting is the accurate knowledge of those elements that constituted past environments, those that make up the present and those that will mould the future. Armed with that knowledge, the economist will be able to predict the reaction and thus the behaviour of the populace.

Regardless of political dogma, all leaders make the same claim of entitlement to equality of opportunity. People are encouraged to believe that they are each entitled to a similar share of the cake. Politicians introduce a mass of theories, mechanisms and systems designed to balance the vast lump of wealth created by a nation with an equally vast pile of assorted slices which purports to represent the division of the whole between all those entitled to its enjoyment. Where the slices are obviously unequal, equality is then defined as that of relativity with contribution, effort or need according to the gospel of those in charge.

The task is impossible and is known to be such. Indeed, if it could be successfully concluded it would signal the end of incentive,

17

motivation and the politician. As far as the latter is concerned, he needs dissatisfaction and the economic friction of frustrated choice. As far as the economy is concerned, it must progress and that is determined by change which in turn depends upon pressures for and against, namely conflict. Self-satisfaction is the precursor of obesity with all that that implies, including a premature death.

Statistics have become the personalised weapons of the politicians. Some use them as rapiers, carefully selected, thrust in and out before their validity can be questioned. Others brandish figures like cutlasses, with broad sweeps to mow down all opposition. Almost without exception, their invalidity is by omission. It is the definition, dimension or qualification that may be left out that gives the lie. It is the incomplete statement or the attempt to compare the incomparable that leaves the electorate bemused and ignorant.

Substantive and comprehensive data are confined, if they are used at all, to environmental and strategic analyses and even then the bias in and method of collection need to be questioned. The apparently simple matter of recording and reporting to the U.K. balance of physical trade is subject to such significant retrospective adjustment that considerable doubt is cast upon the accuracy of the conclusions drawn when they are initially published — the time when they should be of the greatest value.

Economists have yet to determine the principles and purpose of statistical analyses to enable them to decide upon the optimum methods best suited to forecasting and assisting in the making of national and international economic decisions regardless of political preferences. The economists' contribution to society is to provide the recipe for the most attractive cake that a nation can bake. They are only interested in its division into slices in so far as the distribution may affect future recipes. To the extent that the consumption of politically determined slices could affect future environments, their interest is justified.

No single pattern of economic behaviour can be considered in isolation. All patterns are inter-related and the theory of relativity is as apposite to economic behaviour as to any other activity within the known universe. The successful entrepreneur is the one who identifies correctly the consequences of some act or event many miles or even years away and their impact upon the environment in which he may be interested.

One attribute not displayed in economic behaviour is that of logic. The simplistic and natural reaction of the individual is not at all indicative of the probable reaction of the crowd towards an identical set of circumstances. The emotion and motivation of the mass are not the summation of its constituents. It has been demonstrated time and time again that even the secret votes of individuals differ from their public assertions. It can therefore be reasonably assumed that intentions and logic are no guide to the future. The only reasonable indicator is the assessment of reaction in the past to similar conditions. The important factor is a correct assessment of what people did and the circumstances in which they did it. Any attempt at motivation analysis is irrelevant. It is literally anyone's guess as to why people do that which they do. It is therefore a waste of time to attempt identification of motives in the vain hope of being able to apply such knowledge gainfully in the future.

Fear is undoubtedly the most powerful human motivator. People are inclined to worry more in anticipation than in the actual sufferance and resolution of a problem. The unknown, by its very nature, is the essence of fearfulness. It follows that broadcasting an interpretation of a future possibility will generate an inordinate reaction. It is difficult to inject confidence when the argument is based solely upon opinions and he who shouts first and loudest will be heard and heeded.

People in the mass are more easily controlled in a strange environment and tend therein to respond to direction to maintain the comfort of contact with each other. The passage across the desert was more easily accomplished than the collection and abstraction from the old or the inhabitation of the new land.

Non-Discretionary Environment

The economic activity of man is determined primarily by those elements outside his control or influence. His only protection against them is knowledge. If he is aware of such elements and is capable of assessing their probable effect, and more particularly their timing, then at the very least he is in a position to take some steps towards the alleviation of any detrimental effect they might have on his standard of living. He may also identify certain other elements in his environment over which he may exercise some control or influence. The first may be defined as non-discretionary and the second as semi-discretionary.

A simple example of a non discretionary element will clearly indicate its relevance and importance in economic analysis. As far as a farmer is concerned, however effective and technically competent his agricultural systems, the weather over which he has no control will determine the limits of his profit or loss. The probability of a disastrous earthquake or even a localised war such as undertaken in the Falkland Islands can over-ride the very best intentions and the planning of economic effort.

Accurate forecasting of non-discretionary events is not only the cornerstone of economic planning, it constitutes the whole of its foundation. Such events determine the parameters within which the economist has to work and to a very large extent the priority of allocation of resources.

It is one of the great tragedies of democratic government that the resources needed to collect, collate and evaluate such knowledge are available only for limited four/five year cycles as politicians alternate and have but temporary command of such resources. A further and human distortion is that the information gained is then interpreted according to political rather than economic objectives with particular regard for the advantage of one segment of society as compared with that of the whole. Indeed it has not been unknown for politicians to suppress information relating to future non-discretionary developments which could be used by their opponents to their disadvantage. A nation can only grow and exploit the opportunities that abound outside its community if its leaders seek, identify and interpret such opportunities with objectivity and integrity. Since the major potential for a nation lies outside its boundaries, it follows that growth and prosperity is derived from extending horizons rather than self examination and contemplation. Growth generated and supported from within is stunted either by incest or introspection.

Lessons from the Past and Present
for the Future

Industry

Industry in the United Kingdom offers a source of never ending
wonder and bewilderment. It is almost inconceivable that a nation
that prides itself on its conservatism and caution should have
generated so many entrepreneurs who have committed hari-kari
with monotonous regularity. Perhaps the leader of the lemmings
has no alternative to being first over the edge of the cliff simply
because he cannot avoid the rush of those who follow. The lessons
are clearly to be seen and are as clearly ignored.

The consistency of industry life cycles is almost without
exception and eliminates any necessity for citing numerous
examples. The similarity of experience is so close that it is quite
practicable to encapsulate the rise and fall of a typical U.K.
manufacturer into a profile that will apply equally to a large
number of disparate industries. These might range from cotton,
wool, motor cycles and machine tools through foundries, potteries
and musical instruments to cutlery, ball and roller bearings, motor
cars, railway rolling stock and printing — the list is almost without
end. The only significant difference between them was their length
of life and swiftness of demise.

In the beginning, the entrepreneur recognised an opportunity
and was able to identify available resources that he could apply in
the profitable satisfaction inherent in that opportunity. A
conservative and cautious start created a sound foundation. Costs
were constantly scrutinised and control was miserly. Labour was
manipulated and managed in isolated pockets.

Carefully controlled growth established substantial profits
which were reflected in physical assets. Reputations gained the
hard way and derived from highly specialised knowledge were
jealously guarded. The combination of a successful past, acres of

buildings and even self-contained communities encouraged complacency and a certainty of continuity. Specialisation, the strength of the past, became the limitation of the future. Long order books inspired confidence and security. Prices related to costs and profits were enhanced by the omission of depreciation and the costs of machinery replacement by continuing to operate outdated plant on the grounds that it still operated effectively — and employed people. Design and development were the outcome of practical experience and the product was built to last. It had to have integrity. The over-riding assumptions were that since all was well, all would remain well, that the technical and commercial know-how had taken decades if not centuries to acquire so that would-be competitors could never catch up. Overseas competitors were not even in the same race. It was left to British companies to vie with British companies for the same customer. Government after government exhorted and praised the exporter but failed dismally to provide the services and support that were actually applicable.

Then the inevitable happened. Past strengths became current weaknesses. Competitors entered markets which had been so assiduously created and served, promptly offering better value for money and/or better services. The failure to invest profits in new technology and processes had come home to roost.

Delivery and service had long taken second place to price although distant markets had consistently made known their preference. The unthinkable had happened. The nation that led the world in motor cycles, potteries, engineering, etc., etc., etc., had itself disappeared over the edge.

Yet if the pattern was so clear and so repetitive why had industries which had the benefit through the passage of time of example ignored the lesson depicted by their deceased forebears? The answer can only be a hotch-pot of emotions that have no economic justification. Long established industrial success cultivates pride, self-confidence, complacency and misplaced certainty. Life is comfortable for those who have the responsibility for decision making and can only be upset by the self-imposed discomfort of deliberate change.

Almost without exception, the economic behaviour of man in the United Kingdom since the Industrial Revolution has followed the profile of the product life cycle. There has been no attempt to pre-empt that cycle. There has seldom been any acknowledgement that decline must occur. That challenge has never been accepted. Man has continuously reacted to his environment until there is no choice and the decision is forced upon him. The feat of pre-emption is not that of possible error or even defeat. It is that of ridicule and unpopularity.

The United Kingdom has lost literally scores of highly prosperous industries as well as the resources and capabilities of many overseas lands, so it would appear extremely unlikely that, at this stage, Britain will be able to avoid repetition in the years ahead. It will need external pressures or forces to eliminate the time lag between the product/industry life cycle pattern and the behaviour pattern of Management. These could be exerted by the Japanese or at some later stage the Chinese. The British philosophy is that self destruction is regrettable but cushioned by the fact that failure satisfies the envy of those who have observed the rise and fall. But aggression from without is quite another matter and totally unacceptable. Self-defence unifies and justifies almost any sacrifice, even the consequences of pre-emption and change. So British salvation may still lie in reaction to the rays of the rising sun.

Commerce

Commerce is usually regarded as synonomous with industry. This is not necessarily so and the study of commerce merits a separate endeavour.

Commerce and service have long been recognised by the "foreigner" as the true strengths and opportunity areas for the United Kingdom. The British have never accepted that contention, much preferring to point to railways, vehicles and physical goods as more acceptable evidence of their capabilities. The assumption that their strength lay in manufacturing satisfied their ego and to that they clung. In this they were encouraged by the politician who sought votes by appealing to national pride and non-contentious matters, by entrepreneurs who sought cheap labour and by overseas competitors that wished to exploit the commercial markets of the world and avoid intervention by the British.

It is very satisfying to be able to touch the result of one's endeavours, particularly when it will be acknowledged by many as a monument. By unanimous consent, the British were good at making things, so that is what they did.

In truth, the British were no better than the French in making aircraft, no better than the Germans in making cars, no better than the Italians in civil engineering — in short they were no better than most of their direct competitors and not as good as some. They did, however, have one distinct advantage which within a few decades had become an encumberance. The British had been longer at it than most and enjoyed vast resources and cheap labour. Unfortunately these advantages had to be discarded and the British were unable to release them for fear of falling before they had grasped new ropes. They were left swinging aimlessly.

Napoleon had it right. Mrs. Thatcher had it right when she moved into office, but by 1987 it is more than likely that she will have abandoned her policy in favour of the better vote collecting stance of manufacturing resuscitation and reduction of unemployment. Yet Britain is indeed a nation of shopkeepers. The British are second to none in the provision of trading services which lubricate the transition of all the resources needed for production as well as the capabilities required for consumer satisfaction. The United Kingdom could offer the world a complete package of services which would enable those countries which have unique natural resources to maximise the return from their sale right through to the ultimate consumer who could also be assured of satisfaction.

The apparent impediment is unemployment. The simplest political solution would be to put Britain back to work. That can only be achieved in economic terms by repeating the mistakes of the past. In order to employ physically the vast majority of its working population in the manufacture of goods, Britain would have to forego investment in automation, robotics or any major labour-saving devices. Jobs would have to be recreated that utilise the skills taught over the last two centuries. Employment conditions would continue to be unacceptable in attempts to reduce overheads, thereby ensuring the continued influence of Trade Unions. In theory, sweat shops would be ideal. In fact, the whole concept is ludicrous. Nevertheless there are some manufacturing industries in which Great Britain can still compete economically and these will continue and justify investment. They will not, however, create a vast demand for labour.

To resolve unemployment politically at any price economically is to light the very short fuse of an extremely potent bomb. It is no answer to anything other than an anarchist's prayer.

The alternative strategy is to lead the nation deliberately and as swiftly as is practicable into the provision of trading services which will provide some additional jobs, but more importantly increase overseas earnings.

The medium and long-term solution to unemployment is the maximisation of added value earned outside the United Kingdom. The advantages are substantial. Services require less investment so that they can earn the same return in absolute terms as a much larger investment in the production of goods. The higher the return in relative terms to investment, the faster the growth and with that the greater the increase in absolute terms. The result is a significant increase in national wealth, albeit not represented in premises, plant and machinery.

Added value earned overseas produces a dual value in the form of foreign currency that constitutes a commodity. The other advantages identified in the Japanese international strategy are also applicable. Indeed, the role of the international service centre for world trade is that which the United Kingdom needs to adopt if it wishes to protect itself from the otherwise inevitable domination of world trade by the Japanese post 1990.

A trading nation that can provide efficient service to overseas customers can afford "unemployment". It is preferable to afford "unemployment" than to pay for it by the creation of uneconomic jobs to occupy people and to continue outdated inefficient manufacturing processes that cannot even support themselves let alone make additional wealth to protect the future.

Trading services have never followed the life-cycle of manufacturing industry for the reason that the initiative in the behaviour pattern is with the service entrepreneur. The design, development, production and marketing of a product is not only a lengthy cycle in itself, it also crystalises an inflexible investment with a finite life.

The initiative is soon lost by the manufacturing entrepreneur who can only react to environmental changes slowly and with increasing difficulty.

The provision of services, where the original capability already exists, can be developed, moulded and amended with considerable flexibility. The service entrepreneur has the opportunity of leading rather than following.

Services are not necessarily labour intensive so even with their success, employment will not expand dramatically. Nevertheless, as more and more countries seek to transform their natural resources into finished goods, the world demand for services must increase. The outcome should be increased wealth and prosperity for the nation as a whole and far greater opportunity for the individual in the years ahead.

It would be easy to dismiss the human problems which arise when men and women are unemployed and it would appear almost inhuman to suggest that society could regard a significant proportion of its workforce as permanently without work. Stripped of idealistic imagination the alternatives in reality, let alone in economic terms, provide a clear preference. The conditions of employment in labour intensive studies in the United Kingdom had very little to commend them as an environment for the development of individuals as human beings. The main object of work was to earn sufficient reward to enjoy a standard of living for which people were conditioned. The fact that standards were too low has already been forgotten.

The challenge facing the United Kingdom is not to put the clock back and return to the bad old good old days. Britain has the economic resources, the capability and the opportunity whereby it may within a generation fufill the promise that has been proferred by politicians for decades as carrots never intended for consumption.

Exports

To the victors, the spoils — and the spoils in 1945 were reparations from Germany to the U.K., the delight of the entrepreneur.

British businessmen were not slow to take advantage of the situation. They eagerly transhipped plant, tools and dies which they knew were capable of producing goods that had been world-leaders of their kind in 1939.

From 1945 to 1955, the British Government enthusiastically exhorted the entrepreneur to export his output. Purchase tax was levied, sometimes at the rate of 100%, in a fiscal attempt to discourage home consumption and force entrepreneurs to turn overseas for their markets. Manufacturing was the means whereby the nation would recapture its former glory. The fact that it did matter what was sold and to whom was irrelevant. The world was the oyster.

The logic appeared irrefutable. But the consequences, although inevitable, were the exact opposite of expectations. Countries that had been laid low and countries that were setting out along the path of industrialisation had one aim in common. They needed the basic tools to construct an industrial society with its attendant infrastructure. They required transport, machine-tools, diesel generators and all the ingredients for a sound foundation. That the British provided. Then they needed, in the case of developed countries, to resuscitate their capabilities and capacity. During that period of expansion they purchased consumer goods — supplied again by the British.

When, however, the foundations were ready for their superstructure, the former enemies and allies looked to their own initiative to design, develop and produce the most modern and efficient equipment. Their first advance along their predetermined paths was to secure their respective home markets. The Germans achieved this by adopting the reverse of the British policy. Whereas the latter maintained high domestic prices and low export prices, the Germans offered their domestic customers quality goods at low prices and relied upon quality to secure their potential export markets. The net result was success for the Germans. The British even had difficulty in defending their own doorstep as the reputation of the German products became known. Established German factories had preference over their British counterparts when multi-national companies came to decide upon production location. The United Kingdom suffered the ultimate indignity of importing German made goods manufactured on behalf of British subsidiaries of American parents, a fate glossed over by politicians replete on oil revenue. As for overseas markets, the British were often forced to give best to quality, reliability and service. The Germans had effectively established a protected home market and exploited the weaknesses of a vague British export policy.

The United Kingdom had taken the obvious and easier road to recovery and riches. It had put the quantity of overseas earnings before all other considerations. Its export policy was simply to make domestically and sell abroad. There had been no plan of campaign other than that directed towards the short-term maximisation of exports. British international economic policy was

27

no more than an exact facsimile of its national economic policy which was itself an identi-kit of individual industry policies.

The behaviour pattern was determined by events and completely reactive. There were no environmental studies and no projection of the probable strategies of future competitive nations. Britain's policy between 1945 and 1965 could not have been more effectively designed if the objective had been to use its national resources and capabilities for the liberal and selfless recovery of industrial nations in the Western Hemisphere. Whilst providing their means, it had omitted to refurbish itself. But above all, the British had lacked the dedicated and consistent economic leadership that other nations, such as Germany, France and Japan, enjoyed. No country can expect to succeed when its overseas marketing policy is unplanned, uncoordinated and unrelated to an overall economic strategy.

Looking to the future, the United Kingdom still has no international economic policy free of party dogma. Its efforts in earning foreign currency remain fragmented and opportunistic. It is no longer a question of staying with the leading bunch of runners. Britain is struggling to stay in the race. Now, as never before, the country desperately needs a comprehensive strategy and consistent leadership in its application. Whether that is practicable in a democracy is debated elsewhere, but if it is not practicable then the choice is either a continuance of economic decline occasionally arrested by opportunistic advantages or an honest review of the means and methods of government and the needs of society. Democracy will remain as it is and will never approach that which it should be. If what it is is misrepresentation, then there might still be hope for change and with that the responsibility of economic leadership.

Summary

Britain has many excuses for its failure to make the most of all the advantages it has had, starting with the historic inevitability of decline and fall and finishing with the human fear of the unknown.

There is no point in attempting to apportion blame or responsibility. It is equally futile to explore motivation. Knowledge of the past is of positive value for the future only in the elimination of self-deception and as an incentive to prepare for the future. Britain obviously cannot afford to go on wasting resources and opportunities. To survive and prosper, the nation must explore objectively and with integrity the probable alternatives open to it and then have the courage to take a series of predetermined steps, each of which is uncertain and confirmed only after commitment.

To move forward in the dark firmly but carefully is to become aware of the dangers and to avoid them. To stand still is self-deception and simply to wait unprepared for the unknown — and that when it identifies itself can be very unpleasant.

Economic Policy and Economic Philosophy

When the politician has succeeded in extracting power from the populace, he is faced with the task of constructing a policy which he believes will satisfy most of the obligations he has undertaken. His policy sets out a course of action that seeks to use resources and opportunities to achieve the fulfilment of political promises which may or may not be economically desirable or even practicable. And there lies the rub.

Politically based economic policies are almost always incompatible with a prudent course of economic action. Yet that conflict must continue as long as democracy is the agreed form of government. Promises will be made and policies adapted to fit them. Policies will continue to be inadequate and constantly amended. The nation will veer from one course to another with very little direct progress.

In such conditions, if a nation is to survive and prosper in the future, it is essential that it should at least have established an Economic Philosophy which, published or not, will provide a constant thread of effort and achievement, that can absorb policy deviations and identify the corrective courses of action that may be needed to resume the agreed heading.

Economic policy should be a prudent plan of action, using resources and exploiting current opportunities to maximise a nation's wealth.

Economic Philosophy is a statement of the ultimate reality of achievement and is the outcome of experience. Policies are changed, but Philosophy evolves. Policies are clouded by political expediency. Philosophy is concernerd with the body politic.

Policy is the banner of the professional politician. Philosophy is the standard of the statesman.

Philosophy can be stated in simple terms, but its translation into reality and practical implementation has substantial and complex implications.

All democracies need clearly defined individual Economic Philosophies and some, whilst not by any means admitting thereto, have already demonstrated their existence. For example:

Germany's Philosophy — to dominate Europe economically through the re-unification of West and East Germany.

Japan's Philosophy — to control the global creation of wealth.

France's Philosophy — to be a totally self-contained, therefore, independent, and wealthy nation.

In these countries, whichever political party may be in power, whatever pre-election promises may have been made, policies are not allowed to impede the ultimate realisation of these aims. There is national agreement that internal differences and problems are temporary matters that can be resolved without affecting the overall objective. Economic Philosophy over-rules economic policies. Economic Philosophy reigns until it attains.

The United Kingdom needs an Economic Philosophy if it is to avoid being overwhelmed by countries who know where they are going. Whilst they may not succeed totally in their endeavours, their progress will still be significant when compared with that of Britain who will have achieved little more than that which has been handed to it on a plate.

It would appear that an Economic Philosophy has three essential elements:

1. An international strategy.

2. A wealth maximisation strategy consistent with continuity.

3. An internal division of wealth policy.

All the elements are inter-related and are continuously reviewed solely to test the original assumptions and not the intent. Translating that theory into practice, it may well be considered appropriate for the United Kingdom to adopt the following elements in its Economic Philosophy.

1. The creation of an industrial and commercial world trade service centre.

2. Substantial investment in resources of all kinds outside its national borders.

3. Those who contribute to the wealth of its society are rewarded with a significant proportion of their contribution during their lifetime. Those who have not been in a position to assist in wealth creation still benefit directly from the improvement of the standard of living derived from the contribution of those who have. Since the effect of this policy is that the wealth of a nation is consumed by its people, disposition and inheritance is eliminated and that may prove an unacceptable price to some. An immediate example of the contentious nature of the decision determining the division of the spoils, which nevertheless remains the least important element in a nation's Economic Philosophy.

In the years ahead, each successive government would compare the policies arising from their respective party manifestos with the agreed Economic Philosophy. Where there appeared to be direct conflict with the first two elements of the philosophy, amendments would be introduced to avoid a loss of course. To suggest that this would be dishonest or politically unacceptable would be naive. Policies seldom reflect accurately election promises and when they do they never lead to their satisfactory fulfilment. There is in fact only one hurdle and that is an all-party agreement as to that which is best for the nation as a whole, the specification of the size and constituents of the national cake together with the method of its baking.

An agreed international Economic Philosophy does not diminish political opportunities. Its third element provides more than enough to satisfy the most ambitious and power hungry. Whilst it remains the third element of the total Philosophy, it is an arena for personal satisfaction that the country can afford.

The main problem will be one of disclosure. As far as the United Kingdom is concerned, its economic policy should be determined by its political rulers' appreciation of future environmental opportunities and their ability to identify the optimum mix of the resources at its disposal to create wealth. Its Economic Philosophy is not so easily defined since at present it is a conglomeration of platforms cnstructed by politicians each with the sole objective of gaining popular support. In a democracy, it is not enough to state simply that the nation's objective is to become once again a leading power in the world. The cynical could point backwards in time and ask what benefits were derived by the greater proportion of the country's inhabitants when that condition actually existed. Democracy demands a simple response to the individual's question of "What's in it for me?" since that is the enticement of all political promises. It follows, therefore, that at the present time the Economic Philosophy of the United Kingdom is little more than the learning process of its leaders whose public utterances must be confined to promises and thereby to policies. The introduction of an Economic Philosophy without publication would not only lead to a charge of conspiracy and duplicity, it would also leave the way open to a return to the current economic anarchy and confusion, a temptation that sooner or later would prove irresistable to an elected politician.

A superficial assessment of the actions of the Thatcher government might lead to the suspicion that it has already imposed a national strategy at which all other policies must bow the knee. Further examination would suggest that whilst that government has developed a general political philosophy in its approach to internal affairs, it has not attempted to create a truly internationally based Economic Philosophy. That conclusion is wholly compatible with its relationships with the U.S.A., Japan, France and Germany whose international policies dominate those of the United Kingdom.

The wealth of a nation is determined by the ability of its leadership to assess correctly its potential opportunities and to organise resources to take advantage of them at the right time. Wealth itself is the accumulation of added value achieved at successive points of time by opportunistic application of resources. The value of wealth in each discrete segment is determined by the success or otherwise of the then current economic policy. Without a constant thread of Economic Philosophy not only is the continuity of wealth accumulation in jeopardy, but it is unlikely that even the short-term opportunities will be maximised.

A country may have to change its immediate course of action

from time to time. Its ultimate reality and therefore its Economic Philosophy must remain constant.

In the twentieth century, the main impediment in maximising the wealth of a nation is its internal political intervention. The strength and effectiveness of this interference varies from one country to another and is determined by the ability of those who intervene seeking power to maintain and increase social demarcations, class divides and religious conflicts. Political intervention can be defeated by statesmen whose weapons are not dissimilar to those of the politician. The statesman must appeal to the three baser motives of man. He must still make promises. But the significant difference between the politician and the statesman is that the former can and will adjust his argument even to the point that he may never arrive at any destination. The adjustments of the statesman must be compensatory. He not only knows where he is going, he is absolutely determined that his country is going to get there.

Consequently, the statesman faces two dangers. His constancy, integrity and even his oratory may be overwhelmed by the attraction painted by his political opponents in times of discomfort and in the absence of results. His security of office is as tenuous as the gullibility of man. By far the greater danger, is himself. The statesman is but human. He may be wrong and the destination may not be worth the journey and that he will never know.

Economic Planning

By the end of 1986 the profile of the United Kingdom economy bore no resemblance to any previous description. The country was producing a significant proportion of the world's output in oil which it sold for dollars. Its manufacturing industry had been decimated. The U.K.'s activities in services had expanded but had made little impact on unemployment which was substantial both in absolute and relative terms. The average age of the unemployed was appallingly low and the proportion of long-term unemployed disastrously high.

The government had to contend with a complex position with no advantage whatsoever to be gained from past experience.

The first problem had been the conflict between the desire for strong sterling and the wish to enjoy a large dollar income. The lower the value of sterling the greater the benefit from oil/dollar revenues. Then there had been a conflict between the increased cost of imports and the opportunity for exports both directly attributable to weak sterling. Finally, the reduction in consumer goods manufacturing had led to a dependence upon a large proportion of imported as against manufactured items so that the cost of living was affected more dramatically and quickly by changes in rates of exchange. The U.K. economy had become more sensitive to external factors than ever before but, and it is a most significant qualification, it had one major element of influence under its direct control, namely the production of oil.

Interest rates had become a secondary consideration and served only to sustain short-term movements in external rates of exchange. Their impact upon costs of living statistics was less adverse than the reduction in costs occasioned by cheaper imports brought about by strong sterling. The elimination of some manufacturing facilities had shortened the time between cause and effect. Whereas previously import costs had related mainly to raw materials that had to be processed and took an inordinate time to work through the system before affecting the consumer, post 1985 variations in costs of finished imported goods surfaced very rapidly in a much more competitive environment. Consequently the Conservative government gave political preference to reduction in the cost of living and discounted the importance of interest rates, secure in the knowledge that it had the massive advantage that dollar production (which was the true output of the North Sea) was substantial enough to finance the transition from a manufacturing to a trading nation. The cost of unemployment was covered by the translation of fixed assets into working assets or more simply, privatisation. Accounting techniques were used in local government financial controls to give the appearance of accord with political promises.

The critical factors in planning are always time and timing. In the short term British national resources and global trade recession provided sufficient economic and political credibility to enable the government to weather an otherwise overwhelming storm. But the rigging was not compatible with long-term prospects. Oil is a depreciating asset. Realisation of fixed into current assets is only a change of nomenclature unless the assets actually earn more (in the form of taxes on increased profits). The emergence of the U.K. as a profitable trading enterprise had to happen before its assets had been dissipated and that is unlikely if only because of the lack of return from a high proportion of its labour force.

It will be reasonable to assume that in the absence of unforeseeable external events that the race will be lost. It will be found that the United Kingdom is unable to create surplus wealth to replace the income presently derived from oil. The consequences of this failure are obvious and hardly need restating. The country will degenerate into a European off-shore tax and service haven.

The one possibility eagerly pursued by the Conservative government has been the potential of the City as an income earner. The City has been encouraged by the fallout from privatisation and the deliberate disregard of its manipulative and massaging but profitable practices. The inhabitants of the golden mile police themselves and it is patently obvious that the value of their contribution to the economy of the U.K. deters political intervention except in the most outrageous published malpractices.

It is quite clear that in addition to a laissez-faire governmental attitude, if the City is to become and remain a centre for international trading, it will need the appropriate resources. That necessitates the availability of very large sums of money that can only be offered by similarly large organisations. It is likely therefore that in the near future the City will be dominated by a small number of internationally controlled entities who can command the magnitude of capital required. These corporations will be well beyond the control of the U.K. politicians and even if they were not, it is unlikely that a British government would risk strangling the goose, as has already been demonstrated in their negotiations on trade relations with Japan. That which was intended to become a very substantial wealth creator for the benefit of the British exchequer may well offer the U.K.'s main competitors the last vital link in their Economic Philosophy.

It would not be so far-fetched to suggest that one day not far hence, the tail may wag the dog and once again we will have a prime example of the law of political economic inversion. What was introduced as a political expediency to achieve an economic aim actually produces precisely the opposite. The City, supported and dominated by international corporations could well become the trading centre of the world, but the benefit derived by the nation may be beyond the influence of the nation's government and entirely at the whim or fancy of those who compete with us. An economic objective can only be achieved through economic decisions taken and implemented without political bias.

There is need in the country's forward planning for an element which in 1986 may be present but not acknowledged as a feature of the country's strategy.

There is a logical approach to the identification of such an element which has been used with considerable success in the field of company corporate planning. It is based on the principle of Distinctive Competence.

The Distinctive Competence of a country is that combination of attributes that it possesses which makes that country different from any other.

In examining what a country has in terms of assets and capabilities, the intent is to construct a profile. Just as in the case of an individual person, each country has certain dominant features. Yet each profile is unique. A number of countries may have the same dominant features but no two countries will have exactly the same combination. This is because the characteristics are identified in order of significance. There is also a relativity between the characteristics. It is the total combination and respective relativity which makes each profile unique.

It is not difficult to exemplify this approach in terms of an individual by simply listing his facial features. If a similar exercise is carried out for a number of people the result is a number of profiles or caricatures which in the eyes of those who constructed them represent quite clearly the features of the people involved.

A profile constructed by one individual of himself will be markedly different from that constructed of him by another. Others seldom see us as we see ourselves. This can lead to an obvious potential problem as to which profile is correct. Acknowledgement of that possibility confirms the contribution that can be made by an onlooker and the need for a totally objective assessment. The main hurdle to be overcome in identifying the Distinctive Competence of a country is the need for absolute integrity. That is exemplified at a very early stage in the process of examining a country's Distinctive Competence and its own future.

Every country has certain abilities, certain inherent aptitudes, some of which have been inherited and some of which have been developed. Sometimes these abilities have never really been used, and quite often where they have been utilised there has been no recognition of the fact. Inevitably, such abilities are related to people.

The purpose of planning is to ensure the long-term opportunity for growth. Its starting point is what is. It is concerned with what will be.

The immediate task of identifying resources provides a means of assessing the degree to which they are being used and what can be done to improve their utilisation under current conditions. In short, that it should be possible to enjoy the best that can currently be obtained from endeavours and resources.

The next task is to evaluate the potential for the current Distinctive Competence. Inevitably the result will be a rapid reduction in wealth creation through the application of a static combination of resources to an ever-changing pattern of demand and competitive supply.

The sequence can therefore be summarised as follows:

1. A country's Distinctive Competence represents a profile of aptitudes, capabilities and resources in order of significance. Its re-analysis will establish whether the constituent elements have individual development potential. If this is so then the profile will be flexible, and it will be possible to create a new Distinctive Competence out of the available resources. This is a valuable exercise involving relatively little external assistance and can be remarkably elastic. It must in the first instance be carried out independently of the knowledge obtained in the opportunty projection exercise in order to avoid bias. It must obviously be unaffected by political dogma.

2. The second phase requires a creation of a potential Distinctive Competence which consists of latent aptitudes, capacities and resources which by definition are irrelevant to the current environment needs but are available for development.

3. Both sets represent alternative strategies and these can now be aligned with the environmental projections.

The most important, and difficult factor in planning is the identification of the future environment. An increasing proportion of that environment will be defined as non-discretionary. Whether a country likes it or not, it will have to accept conditions which are imposed upon it and which will limit its opportunities and indeed its sovereignty. It follows that non-discretionary elements have to be forecast with a reasonable degree of accuracy and it is in that activity that by far the greatest proportion of research investment must be directed.

It is one thing to pontificate on principles and theories. It is quite another to translate them into practical examples. However, there is one element in the current U.K. Distinctive Competence profile that merits consideration as a possible dominant feature in the early twenty-first century. It accords with the principle that it is, in fact, a latent strength and therefore requires relatively little new investment. It is also a feature that is more widely recognised and valued by those outside the United Kingdom. Its development has both direct and indirect advantages and constitutes a potentially substantial overseas investment. That element is academic education.

Concentration upon training schemes designed to equip young people for work that is incompatible with the U.K. economy of the future will have wasted both resources and opportunity. The irony will be that that which has long been regarded as the jewel in the crown of British institutions will have been sacrificed in the short term on the altars of political expediency and economic myopia.

Academic education is particularly apposite for a nation that has decided its future is in service industries, training and the overseas investment of expertise. No-one can doubt the potential rewards of a system which can influence the minds of those who will take the decisions of the future in countries of all shapes and sizes.

That which is erudite today is commonplace tomorrow in the fields of research and development. The speed of technological evolution is so great that academic abstraction will be in great demand in the twenty-first century. But there is another dimension, the reaction of society to economic war and the revolution in work, its redefinition and the consequences arising therefrom.

Again, much has been said about the preparation for leisure. Little has been done about it and industry has had neither the inclination or the leadership to accept direct involvement in the social problems arising from the reduction in the proportion of time spent on necessary economic pursuits. Yet the social revolution cannot be isolated from the technological revolution. Acceleration in the latter adds to the pressures on the former. The catalyst could well be academic excellence.

It is probable that the pattern of behaviour of man in the mass will determine the U.K. profile almost despite the protestations, ambitions and efforts of the politicians, unless the United Kingdom does introduce a new emphasis in its future profile.

Without such an element and faced with the clearly defined environment resulting from some fifty years of "peace", the success of foreign economic aggression and the failure of indigenous resource management, the pattern is almost inevitable. It will be one of retraction, segmentation and introvert satisfaction. The national environment may well be comfortable and its inhabitants reconciled with their present and future. It will not, however, be one conducive to challenge since it will be incapable of change.

An extrapolation of what is to what may be in, say, twenty-five years based upon present trends, attitudes and actions is acceptable only for those who fit the politician's dream of moronic acquiescence. As long as leaders have to depend upon transitory support, whatever their ideals and judgement they are forced to take those paths along which they receive the plaudits of their followers who enjoy the ease and comfort of the chosen route.

Such paths are short and expectation exceeds life.

Continuity of political strategy is only possible where the related sources of power will accept short and medium-term inconvenience as a necessary step towards an ultimate goal. The only resources of power who take such a long-term view are those related to land and limited ideology institutions. In the United Kingdom those who own land may well decide that continuity of an economic strategy which they deem desirable is only possible through discontinuity of political tactics. Therefore they will accept periods of office occupied by those superficially antagonistic towards their objectives secure in the knowledge that politicians dependent upon people's support cannot sustain office indefinitely. Further, that whilst such offices are occupied by those of opposing views, the very nature of their tenure will be such as to breed discontent and difficulties which will in turn make the task of the reinstated favoured politician that much easier. In the absence of unforeseen external elements, such will be the pattern for the next twenty-five years as far as the U.K. political leadership is concerned. There will be long periods of Conservative rule linked by much shorter terms of office held by the opposition, whichever party that may be. In the absence of any significant change in the country's economic strategy, the main influence in the early twenty-first century on the United Kingdom's economy will be the effectiveness of Japanese international strategy.

This brings us back to the inclusion of academic excellence as a main plank in the development of the U.K. economy designed primarily to be extended well beyond its boundaries as an investment in every way competitive with the more readily recognised forms of money, technology and trade.

The current Distinctive Competence of the United Kingdom which would be particularly appropriate for the environment envisaged at the end of this century is:

1. An *international* trading and commercial strategy, with particular reference to that of the Japanese.

41

2. An educational policy giving far greater emphasis to *academic excellence* rather than technological competence.

3. A monetary policy which isolates the control and direction of money as an internal medium of exchange from commodity bargaining of money in the form of international currency.

By definition, these are all long-term objectives. The United Kingdom has the advantage that none of the elements requires resources or capabilities which are not present in the national cupboard. The country does not have to go shopping or shoplifting.

Those who can make a valuable contribution are ready, able and willing.

It is one thing to plan correctly. It is quite another to implement effectively. There is no better way of uniting a people than the production of a common foe. Fear is the most powerful motivator and if it can be focussed nothing is impossible. That has been demonstrated time and time again during periods of open warfare.

The people of the United Kingdom have every right to be fearful for their future. Not because of the threat of the atomic bomb or the malaise of internal social revolution. Unless the country can get its economic act together it will, well within half a century, be as impotent as an old-age pensioner and as equally dependent and powerless. The country will then reflect the dominance of a segment of its society that will have no taste for challenge or change.

By far the greatest challenge must be planning for decline. In theory such planning is quite unacceptable, but in practice equally inevitable. To plan for decline is usually taken as acceptance of defeat. It need not be so. Neither is it a question of accepting the inevitable and lying back to enjoy it. It is a rational comprehension of economics and an attempt to use that knowledge to advantage.

Growth cannot continue indefinitely, neither can stagnation survive. Therefore, sooner or later there will be a decline and fall. Ignored, it will not go away. Anticipated, it can be a positive force for the future.

The basic cause of decline is beyond the control of the nation. If this were not so, then it could be avoided. It is usually found in the non-discretionary environment and may be a combination of many related and apparently unrelated factors.

Planning for decline is part of the total economic planning process. Acknowledgement of its existence and effect enables the economist to identify compensatory elements, essential for the continued well being of the nation. Preparation for the inevitable could allow the economist at least to control the rate of descent and hopefully to be able to assess the speed of introduction required for the replacement activity.

A decline in demand creates surplus resources. These resources may have been worked and their value written down. Re-application of their use can therefore offer an extremely attractive economic proposition. But for what purpose? In addition to technological developments, emerging nations can often offer similar outdated resources at far more competitive prices.

In some parts of the United Kingdom, the foundry industry has been literally wiped off the face of the earth. The skills that enabled men to produce almost by hand fine catings at ridiculously low prices are dying with them. So we destroy buildings and equipment for which there is no future, but at the same time we ignore and so eventually destroy knowledge and experience that can be grafted elsewhere and which are an inheritance worthy of retention. Had the decline of the foundry industry been faced as an unavoidable eventual trend, then it is possible that the economists and industrialists could have identified those distinctive elements within the industry that individually, collectively or in combination with those outside the industry either in the present or the future should be retained or even extended. As it was, all was lost and with it some of the seeds for new growth.

There is no loss, of face in planning the inevitable, but to invoke temporary blindness is a Nelsonian feature which mighty few can succeed.

Economic Restrictions and Restraints

A totally free market is both impractical and unacceptable. All markets encourage and suffer restrictions and restraints in one form or another and to varying degrees. These limitations exist to permit and ensure continuity. Unfettered free markets tend to favour the immediate profit irrespective of the long-term effect. The imposition of rules and regulations usually serve to protect those who do not immediately benefit from current transactions. Order and control ensure that there will be a repetitive use of the market over a reasonable period, so that it gains from the cultivated integrity and efficiency of those who utilise its facilities.

Thus the Stock Exchange London imposes many conditions on those who take advantage of its services. And again, international commodity markets observe clearly defined requirements and currency transactions depend upon accepted practices.

There are grounds, other than economic, for intervention. These can be political, religious or humanitarian. The effect of these is seldom that which is intended for several potent reasons. First intervention must lead to conflict, since it is designed to modify the otherwise anticipated outcome of a particular activity. The conflict occasions reaction and since the activity that is under attack is "natural" and fundamental, the reaction is often fierce and positive. Secondly, there is an underlying assumption tht without intervention, the normal economic activities of man will lead to results that are defined as undesirable by those who then wish to interfere. The behaviour pattern is disturbed at the behest of a minority whose grounds are entirely subjective. Then finally, intervention creates the unnecessary risk of uncertainty. If the pattern is modified then the outcome may not conform with the desires of those who intervened. Even when it does, restraint must be sustained to maintain an "unnatural" posture. So the complications are enormous. There can be no guarantee that the intervention will be effective or that the outcome will be that which was intended or, even if it is, that it can be sustained. There is one further aspect that adds to the discomfort. The total cycle of intervention with its immediate and long-term results can seldom be forecast as to shape and pattern because by its very nature it is unlikely to be repetitive.

This is exemplified time and time again by the politician who however experienced he may be, is still unable to devise an appropriate formula which will modify the behaviour pattern of the populace and still achieve the end result which he has publicly proclaimed as desirable.

The same problems arise whatever the grounds for non-economic intervention, but they can vary according to the breadth of view that is taken. The nearer they are to the concept of man as a total entity, the less the economic problems that will be encountered. For example, where religious restraints are introduced to support the weak against the strong or discourage short term profits at the cost of long term health, they can add to the attractions of a given market place and improve its economic prospects. But impositions designed to favour or promote denominational views are invariably detrimental to all those involved or affected. The basic tenets of Christianity can improve the long term well being of man, but it is extremely unlikely that similar results would be achieved from the application of the tracts of any particular branch of that ethos.

Restrictions and restraints upon economic endeavour for humanitarian reasons are notoriously self-defeating, whether in the provision of short term expediences or the imposition of standards. The effect on the prosperity of those on whose behalf the action has been taken is seldom if ever beneficial.

The common feature of all forms of restrictions and restraint other than those that arise because of economic intent is that in the minds of those who intervene or promote intervention their subjective assessment is inevitably prejudiced. They are committed to a point of view that over-rides all other considerations, which by definition must include those that are economic.

Restrictions that are introduced for reasons that may be considered laudatory or morally correct can lead to the most unexpected consequences and actually create economic conditions that are directly to the disadvantage of those on whose behalf the action was taken.

As argued earlier, there must still be some inhibitions applied if only to ensure continuity of investment based on the confidence of an orderly market. Those raise no problems. Equally so, since the economic activity of man is best conducted within an ordered society, he must also accept certain restraints if not for the immediate benefit of himself, then for the advantage of his successors. Again, these do not represent insuperable hurdles and finally, since there is a general belief that the quality of life can be enhanced beyond the economic dimension, it is not difficult to obtain man's co-operation in helping his fellows in need.

Reliance upon "free market forces" is a political expediency. It is based upon the outdated assumptions that freedom of choice is isolated from resources and price is determined where demand equates with supply. Like principles, choice is a matter of what can be afforded. Those with the most have the widest choice. Those with the least may have no choice at all. Those who represent the demand of a very small minority may be forced to accept what was produced to satisfy the needs of the great majority. It may well be correct to say that market forces may be allowed to operate freely, but the catch-phrase must have with it the definition of those market forces which will be applied regardless of consequences other than satisfaction of the return upon investment.

Price is more likely to be determined where the return on capital is acceptable. It is therefore a function of profit and investment. Supply and demand are physical factors that play their part in the equation, but are not final determinants. Indeed, a more significant determinant is confidence. To wait for factual confirmation before completion of a transaction is to offer the competition the opportunity to benefit. As time passes, risk and uncertainty diminish and so does profit. As facts become known, values will crystalise and offer little margin. In fact, price decisions are based more upon experience and the existence of a defensive mechanism to alleviate errors. It is anticipation that determines price and that is a mixture of confidence and an acceptable return upon investment. When a bargain is struck, the value to the buyer is unknown and that is the mark of the entrepreneur. He thinks he knows and hopes to prove it.

Man has many dimensions and needs. Economics are but one. It happens to be the one that affects most of the people most of the time. It is therefore dominant and within the foreseeable future must remain so. Beyond that indisputable fact, there lies a vast area of debate as to its relative significance in the development and improvement of man. There are as many points of view as there are debaters and each is influenced by his lot. Yet there remains one common denominator that whilst it does not eliminate debate certainly keeps the subject clearly in perspective. Man cannot live by bread alone, but without bread he cannot live.

Economic Strategy

Strategy is the science of doing the right thing. Tactics is the art of doing things right. Economists are concerned primarily with strategy. Politicians can only afford tactics. It follows therefore that since politicians rule the day, the United Kingdom's long term economic "strategy" is a combination of accidents and the unavoidable consequences of short term decisions.

It is equally unsurprising to find that political attempts to introduce rules and regulations (known as law by statute) to effect economic policies have more often than not had exactly the reverse effect to that originally intended. This could be defined as the law of the inverse economic certainty which has been consistently applied since 1945.

One example in the U.K. was the introduction of Selective Employment Tax whereby companies were penalised if they employed people. The strategic intent was to force segments of industry which provided services to disgorge "surplus" labour who would then be obliged to accept employment in manufacturing industry, which was acutely short of man-power. The objective was a redistribution of a scarce resource to create greater wealth for all.

The facts at the time were indisputable. Service industries were awash with labour and there was something unpleasant about personal service and tipping which the English socialist found distasteful. The manufacturing employer enjoyed long order books and suffered inadequate output. Above all, Britain was the industrial nation that led the world in a vast selection of goods, from engineering tools to pottery. S.E.T. seemed an obvious solution. It was quickly and firmly introduced. The Inland Revenue need no second bidding in the application and collection of taxes. The politicians assumed their results could be quickly obtained and in that they were right. Their miscalculation, however, was as to the outcome which was exactly the opposite of what they intended for the simple reason that the correct solution to the problem was not in the re-allocation of the scarce resource of labour but the introduction and expansion of the even more inadequate resource of capital.

A more appropriate economic policy would have been to invest substantial finance in manufacturing capacity to reduce the demand for labour, thereby eliminating the need for out-dated skills and accelerating the transition from manufacturing processes and methods designed in the late thirteenth and early twentieth centuries to processes whose only similarity would be in the product finally produced, and even that would be improved. The challenge facing the politicians was, as always, to introduce change before necessity to change arrived. Their inevitable reaction was to rearrange the allocation of one politically sensitive resource and leave everything else undisturbed.

Consequently industries providing services reduced staff and introduced automation. Quality, an inherent characteristic of service, was reduced. Manufacturing industries remained over-manned, capital investment stagnated and production methods continued outdated and inefficient. International competitors could not believe their good fortune and quietly left the United Kingdom floundering in their wake. Britain was left with no alternative. By 1980 it was obliged to concentrate its future on services rather than manufacturing. It is arguable whether that would have been its fate anyway, but whatever the ultimate constitution of its wealth creation mechanism, the transition from the old to the new would have been far less painful socially had the journey been undertaken by planned intent rather than unantici-pated necessity.

One country stands unique amongst the democratic nations in its development and application of a macro economic strategy, Japan.

Japan's strategy has not evolved through government or political policy. It is an extension of the structure, objectives and methods adopted by its industrial society. Japanese industry has benefited from being a late entrant in the Industrial Revolution and the vast investment of American funds after 1945 as atonement for the two atom bombs which in economic terms were wholly justified.

Japanese industry is virtually controlled by its four major banking groups, each of which operates as a separate solar system.

Each system retains its own commercial and industrial bodies which revolve around the central sun. The gravitational pull is simply money. The length and duration of orbit is determined by the success of the individual body in the achievement of its own objectives. Each system has similar bodies within it so that should one part of such a system fail, the galaxy still has some three other contributors to its total welfare.

The structure reflects precisely the characteristics and philosophy of its inhabitants. Industry and commerce are managed by committees who determine the appropriate tactics within quite broad guide lines. Responsibility is shared so that whilst age is still venerated and rewarded, youth is encouraged to make its contribution without literally waiting for dead men's shoes. Strategy on the other hand is determined by a minute number of favoured persons who meet regularly and frequently rather as clubs than as routine boards. Social standards are sufficient to maintain formality. Unlike the United Kingdom, the lack of competition between land and industry has eliminated a class distinction as recognised in Europe so far as economic decision making is concerned.

The approach of its people to the task of wealth creation has enabled them to create a unique and awe-inspiring economic strategy. Some of the Japanese tenets have no parallel in the western hemisphere. They grow from the very roots of their philosophy and have the strength of unconscious acceptability. The obvious attitude of responsibility to country, company and then to oneself as well as an inherent patience, perseverence and stoicism are all well-known and acknowledged. The desire of the Japanese to save face has meant that failure is not for them an orphan. It is simply a temporary impediment from which lessons can be learnt and to that extent provides an invaluable supplement to success. Indeed, the difference between failure and success is only time. The former is momentary whilst the latter is continuous.

Other attributes have had a similar effect upon the fulfilment of Japanese objectives. One such is their attitude to borrowing. The Japanese judge a man's standing by the amount which he can borrow. Obviously he to whom the banks freely lend must have great credit-worthiness. At the same time, very low interest rates permit high volume, low profit margin business. It is preferable to lend large amounts of money at low rates with very little risk and the latter is determined by the desire to save face. Finally, the Japanese as a nation believe in saving.

The consequences are obvious. The banking system virtually controls industry and commerce to the advantage of both. Their objectives are complementary. Industry seeks the largest possible market. It needs substantial investment. Einstein would have been proud of the Japanese model of economic relativity. He would also have seen the potential power of their economic equation.

Every nation that has developed beyond its borders has enjoyed the advantages of its own particular idiosyncracies. It has applied its strengths and pitted them against the weaknesses of opponents. In the early days of man's civilisation, conquest usually depended upon excellence in the martial arts, but as man progressed this had to be supported by organisational ability and leadership, the Romans being the prime example of these capabilities. Their strengths matched exactly the opportunities opened to them. So it is with the Japanese. Their approach to commerce is ideally suited to the challenges of the second half of the twentieth century and, by a strange quirk of fate, their defeat in World War Two provided them with the key resources essential to their long-term strategy.

The pattern of Japanese advance has already been well established. First, they protected their basic market, Japan itself, thereby not only ensuring a huge captive demand but also the ability to regulate the internal standard of living in the preferential use of domestic resources. Secondly, they expanded their manufacturing capacity to satisfy a demand even greater than that represented in Japan. In order to justify this, they invested heavily in market research in potential sources of raw materials and countries that might be encouraged to buy their products. Teams of experts were despatched to many parts of the world, each with clearly defined terms of reference and objectives. On many occasions where the potential was significant, the Japanese employed more than one team in the assessment of a project. Reports would be compared before any decisions were made. In one instance, two such teams investigated the extent and quality of primary materials located in Western Australia and were given every assistance by the State government on condition that they made their findings available to that government. The Australians were obviously interested in the possibility of Japanese investment. When the results were published, their comprehensive nature shook the Australians not a little. In fact they learnt more from the Japanese than they cared to acknowledge. There was no doubt as to the value of the reports and the care taken in their compilation. Despite their depth and comprehension there was still some doubt whether the Japanese kept some conclusions to themselves.

Having acquired the essential knowledge, the next step in the strategy was to design products that would be almost monopolistic in a combination of quality and price. This could be achieved by capturing a segment of a market by offering quality at a highly competitive price. In addition, however, the Japanese insisted upon product support, having examined the weakness of British exports which endeavoured to compete primarily on a price basis. As soon as segment domination had been achieved, prices were increased and more segments attacked until the Japanese products were very well established across the total spectrum of a particular market. A clear example of these tactics was provided in the expansion of the Japanese motor-cycle industry.

Up to this stage, nothing was new. Achievement represented little more than hard work and careful planning. But from there on, the Japanese international strategy was unique and carefully tailored to the changing political and economic conditions of the 1970's and the 1980's. The Japanese were well aware of the problems that would undoubtedly arise from their very success. At the international level, they would be attacked for the consequent imbalance of trade heavily in their favour. At national level, protectionism would emerge in one or more of its many forms in attempts to limit Japanese inroads into individual Western markets.

So the Japanese took steps to pre-empt both. They established manufacturing facilities in developing countries that sought new industries and investment. Such facilities turned out large quantities of goods that, whilst advanced in design, were no more than extensions of those already well established in Japan itself. Within a very few years, products such as ceramics, cameras and electronic domestic items were being made under licence in vast quantities in countries as far apart as the Republic of Ireland, Sri Lanka and Singapore. The Japanese not only benefited from national financial incentives, lower costs, public relations and banking opportunities, they created a method of confusing trade statistics that effectively eliminated the initial political animosity. They increased their foreign earnings, reduced the incidence of tax and above all avoided the congestion of fixed assets which would otherwise have grown like the British topsy with all the eventual problems of the inevitable decline and fall of manufacturing industries. Those problems the Japanese could generously leave with the new owners of the bricks and mortar when they decided that they should move on.

Further advantages accrued from the concentration within Japan upon new technology and new industries which could at some later date be re-allocated in other countries. Meanwhile, the Japanese home market was still closely protected despite promises and more promises regarding its liberalisation. It was not only a question of ensuring even in the most difficult world conditions a continuity of demand for home-produced goods. An essential element of the Japanese strategy was the control of the standard of living in their own country. This was the means whereby they could avoid increased demands for wages and unemployment. The comprehensive satisfaction of a home market by domestically produced goods allowed them to set standards of price and quality and levels of competition. The importation of foreign goods in any substantial numbers would have threatened that capability and undermined their ability to maintain a balance between domestic price and domestic added value. They could afford to maintain a large labour force.

The next stage was to establish manufacturing facilities in developed countries which policy again had many valuable advantages. It was ideal for industries that needed substantial investment. That would be provided by the wet nurse whose inducement would be employment (however minimal) of the indigenous population. The factories would be nicely set up within the very barriers designed to keep the products involved without. No problems with tariffs and quotas. Indeed the goods would bear the mark of the country in which they were produced, adding to the balance of trade confusion. Shipping costs were reduced and "nationally made" articles dominated national markets. Another benefit was derived from the reduction in the otherwise unavoidable import of raw materials into Japan itself. This stage had many advantages of offer, not least being its probable length of effective life. The developed countries would make every effort to continue

53

their production lines. Although in the first instance some goods would be imported from Japan or Japanese controlled industries located elsewhere even these would be offered to the grateful foster parent when the product life cycle was drawing to its inevitable close.

The following phase will undoubtedly take place. The globe is now liberally dotted with Japanese dominated markets, Japanese controlled manufacturing resources and Japanese technological innovation. Eeach dot represents a generator of currency which can flow across boundaries or may be retained in the area in which it is produced. Either way, it creates a web of investment and return over which other countries have little if any influence or control. These sources of money can be used to invest in indigenous industries or indeed in indigenous governments. The potential is enormous. With the advent of "thinking" computers, international currency transactions using twenty-four-hour cycles circling the world and the imbalance created by new media of exchange such as oil, the Japanese monetary empire could command obedience far beyond that accorded to a conqueror whose achievement was by force of arms.

However successful the Japanese strategy may have been or indeed will be, there is nothing to be gained from aping them. The subterfuge of copying was merely the first step taken by the Japanese themselves in order to short-circuit research and development. Their aim has consistently been to produce advanced designs that create and merit their own reputations.

There is little doubt that those responsible for international economic strategies can learn much from the approach and application of the Japanese and other nations of similar singleness of purpose. The principles involved remain the same regardless of the identification and nature of the constituent parts.

The success of any particular strategy is only measureable against its original objective. It is not open to any country to set for itself the target of world domination. It may well be argued that such an aim is the equivalent to national suicide.

An economic strategy is devised to further the well-being of a nation in terms of its wealth. The nation itself has the right to decide the use to which such wealth may be put. An economic strategy must also take into account the perceived competition. Above all, however economic strategy is one of constant evolution adding new objectives as those set in the past are attainable or can be discarded.

The primary factor is the extent of the nation's ambitions. The secondary factors are those beyond the direct control and influence of a nation that might limit those ambitions. A nation's growth has never been limited by the extent of its internal resources. Success has been achieved by the satisfaction of a correctly forecast demand, by the supply of an opportune mix of resources and the defeat of accurately anticipated competition. To know in substance and timing future opportunities and limitations is to be able to plan with assurance and effect. In addition to know oneself is a safeguard of immeasurable value against the unforeseen and the unforeseeable.

The Wealth of Nations

Machiavelli preceded Adam Smith and enjoyed the added advantage of not having the label of an economist. He therefore approached his observations without preconceived notions and the economist's desire to balance all matters, thereby avoiding a finite solution.

Using Machiavellian principles and taking advantage of the passage of time since Smith, it should be possible to re-examine the fundamental question, namely, what is the measurement of wealth of a nation upon which its leaders can rely as one of integrity and usefulness?

It is possible with the benefit of hindsight to establish and compare the behaviour pattern of man in a number of similar circumstances and environments and from that to deduce a practical answer.

Such an example is Singapore.

The first definition of Singapore's wealth was Raffles' recognition of its geographic and geophysical importance. Its natural resources provided its owner with a very valuable asset. It could be very easily converted into a staging post for international shipping. Fortunately for many peoples that recognition was translated into practice, albeit by entrepreneurs rather than governments. Singapore prospered and its wealth was used widely and well. In the absence of a raw material it could not be raped. Whilst it was not paid its correct dues for the services that it offered, its basic wealth remained in a form that could not be abstracted or extracted. The British government continued to use the original Raffles definition of Singapore's wealth up to the time that it abdicated and granted Independence. As far as Parliament was concerned, maintenance of that particular wealth was more costly than the return that could be enjoyed from it.

Mr. Lee Kuan Yew did not suffer from the same tunnel vision. He re-identified and brought a new dimension to Singapore's wealth. He was far-sighted and could see new opportunities to exploit and add to the natural resources of his country. His first plan was to harness the resource of people, previously regarded simply as cheap labour. By educating, training and rehousing he transformed the population within a remarkably short time into a source of potentially proficient people, comparable with any other nation. At first he attracted manufacturing industry but only that which was sophisticated and therefore internationally competitive, not having to rely upon cheap labour to control costs. Then he developed communications over and above those associated with a deep-water port. Next he encouraged international banking and trade services and used the time zone advantage of Singapore for that purpose. Finally, he made plans to take over, in due course, from Hong Kong.

The lessons in Mr. Lee Kuan Yew's progress are clear for all to see. The wealth of a nation lies in its ability to use its indigenous resources suitably trained and/or prepared at the right time to ensure the maximum return. The country's leadership must be far-sighted, flexible, cohesive and coherent. Whatever the physical advantages of a nation, whether they are of location or mineral resources, the essential ingredient in the creation of wealth is the application of its people. The second most important element is that a nation should concentrate upon resources that cannot be depleted. A bonanza of fifty years of oil cannot compare in terms of a nation's wealth with long-term geographical advantages and, above all, the competence and will of its inhabitants.

Another aspect of Mr. Lee Kuan Yew's approach is that he had the ability to stand outside his country and assess what was happening around him. To a certain extent he started with the advantage that Singapore was already a trading link and had long recognised the need for observing closely progress of trade on which it relied. Nevertheless, he could see the opportunities for Singapore in the long-term strategy of Japan. It is probable that more cameras of Japanese design were manufactured in Singapore in 1985 than in the country of Japan itself. He also observed the effect of European Common Market policy upon Australasia and the resultant change in attitude of the Australians so that he incorporated in his strategy certain elements which held out attractions to them. There is no doubt that Mr. Lee has spent considerable time and effort on examining the implications of the long-term strategy of the Chinese Republic and has laid his plans well for trade and commercial relations with them.

It is difficult to over-emphasize the importance of external observation. Growth and prosperity are limited by vision. Vision depends upon where one stands and in which direction one is looking.

An interesting example of this was the evolution and development of what was the largest retailing chain in the United Kingdom. It began in the 1920's, with a struggling shop and a young proprietor working every conceivable hour to survive. Having achieved that he then had time to serve his customers and organise his displays accordingly. The critical point was reached, however, when he stood outside on the pavement, success having enabled him to find the time, and observed those who walked past the shop. His observation allowed him to deduce the formula for the best location for his first branch.

Observation within an environment is essential to know what is needed to get the most out of that which one has. Real growth is only possible when those responsible for its strategy can stand outside that which is and see it for what it is. To look outside from within is to be defensive and of assistance only in consolidation. To stand ouside is to begin to appreciate what one has and what one might have. That is precisely what Mr. Lee Kuan Yew achieved and that which Western politicians have failed so far to appreciate.

In the nineteenth century, the British were directed in the application of their capabilities by a system of local opportunism. As an industrial nation, it was fragmented and ruled by division. The advent of the Great War provided an opportunity for unity of approach and the elimination of those practices which had been almost inhuman. But it was an opportunity missed through the rose-coloured spectacles of victory and the bitter dregs of the 1920's.

It follows, therefore, that the wealth of a nation is determined by its leadership. Latent wealth may provide a feeling of security but is more likely to be a sleeping sickness. It would be difficult to identify any nation that given the appropriate leadership could not enjoy a good standard of living through the exploitation of even very limited resources. The extreme ends of the resource spectrum might be identified as United States of America and the Isle of Man. The first has practically all the raw materials and resources that it could possibly need to establish a very high standard of living for its clients. The second country takes advantage of the needs of its more wealthy brethren and maintains a more than adequate economy.

The rise and fall of nations does not reflect the increase and decline of their wealth.

It is the barometer of effective leadership in that it has failed to identify and use new combinations of old or introduce new resources. Wealth is that which has value at a given time. Change the time and the constituent elements of wealth must change or deteriorate in value.

As long as the definition of a nation's wealth remains constant, then its prosperity will follow the normal product life cycle. Since it is inevitable that that which is in demand today will not be required tomorrow, the wealth of a nation that seeks to maintain a high standard of living is a kaleidoscope of resources the pattern of which is constantly changed by deliberate design in anticipation of the ever-changing environment.

Once again, timing is the key to success. In addition there must be courage as the reallocation and redefinition of resources must anticipate a new pattern of demand. If that anticipation is wrong then the experience will be painful. The alternative, however, of failing to initiate change will be at least as painful and in the long run much more expensive. Stagnation leads to inevitable decline. Transition leading to change has at least an even chance of growth and prosperity.

The National and International Use of Money

Much has been written concerning monetarism and the benefits that might be derived from the control of the volume of purchasing power within an economic system. It was a tool with an obvious cutting edge and welcomed eagerly by the crusading politicians who overlooked the two-edged nature of the blade. As a theory it fell rapidly into disrepute, the inevitable fate in the modern world of any widely acclaimed inanimate object or human being. Whatever its true value, the method and timing of its application ensured its early dismissal.

Monetarism provided a new facade for continuity of the ancient ritual of economic stop-go. During the 1950's and the 1960's this had been achieved metaphorically by the use of the brake and accelerator. During the 1980's, the metaphor emerged as a tap, to be turned on and off according to the level of the liquid in the system.

The stop-go method of control, whether a tap or a brake and accelerator is neither smooth or effective. It is a blind approach, being applied in hopeful ignorance. It assumes that there is one major source of supply. It assumes that the total system will respond in a logical pre-determinable manner based on previous experience. It makes a whole host of assumptions that demonstrate a lack of understanding of the behaviour pattern of people in the mass and the working of industry and commerce in general. It is therefore little wonder that this political interpretation of economic theories has proved disastrous both for driver and passengers.

The object of this book is to be constructive and positive. The temptation to examine the reasons for decline and fall of monetarism will therefore be resisted. Instead, we shall consider the use of money both as to frequency and application.

60

By far the most important characteristic of money its velocity of circulation. This can best be exemplified by the story of a young family, one member of which discovered a penny. With that he purchased from his brother a sweet for which he craved. The next day, that brother purchased a small toy from his sister, who the following day acquired another object from yet another sister. And so on, so that by the end of the week seven transactions had taken place, the Sabbath having been ignored, and the youngsters had been satisfied, some more, some less. By the end of the second week, the excitement had become contagious and the coin now literally flashed from hand to hand so that after a further seven days, the number of transactions far exceeded the number of days. But all good things come to an end, usually when least expected. One day final calamity occurred, the then keeper of the coin lost it. The family was reduced to barter with all its attendant limitations.

Had the lad discovered a sixpence instead of a penny, the economic well-being of his family would not have increased six-fold. Indeed, it might well have suffered. The sixpence might have constituted a surfeit of wealth. The number and unit value in the family system could not have justified a large fund of the exchange medium. After all, a penny had proved quite acceptable so the lucky boy could have hidden five pence for a rainy day. He had little bargaining use for the whole sum and restriction in its availability would enhance its intrinsic value. In any event, the five penny hoard would provide some degree of insurance. High velocity of circulation is vastly preferable to the lethargic sludge of large volumes.

Gresham's Law that bad money will drive out good has been grossly misinterpreted to the disadvantage of modern political monetary policy. The mere fact there is a lack of desire to retain money does not of itself augur ill for a society. On the contrary, money that represents a defensive hoard can be more detrimental than its absence altogether.

Money is the essential element in working capital which is by far the most expensive and effective investment made in industry. Working capital is the link in the economic chain that holds industry together. The way in which one company structures and uses its working capital will have a direct effect upon the approach adopted by those companies linked to it through the debtors and creditors in their structure and in their use of their working capital.

Some links are stronger and more dictatorial than others. The tension that they create to satisfy their individual objectives can strain and ultimately break those that are relatively weak to the detriment of the economy as a whole.

During the first half of the twentieth century, British business prided itself on its ability to pay its debts promptly. The normal terms of trade were payment by the middle of the month following that of delivery of the goods concerned, being a credit cycle of some three weeks. Cash discounts were offered for seven day payment and often taken. Money flowed smoothly between creditor and debtor. Another factor was that bank overdrafts were the exception rather than the rule being regarded as socially unacceptable. Their absence coupled with the general conservative approach towards the management and its valuation of assets encouraged first the asset-stripper and then the credit grabber.

The fiscal policies of successive British governments from the mid 1950's to the mid 1980's accelerated the extension of credit throughout industry. Since working capital represented the most expensive form of investment, the use of creditor's money was extremely attractive as interest on overdue payment of creditors was virtually unknown. Large U.K. companies exploited their strength to create cash mountains that in times of high interest rates earned more than their trading activities.

Everything combined to encourage the asset-stripper whose activity became a socially acceptable means of improving the efficiency of industry, stimulating the economy and benefiting the nation in the use of surplus but previously unrealised value. Borrowing became a way of life for the entrepreneur with high interest rates offset by high rates of taxation. The final political answer to the continued economic problems was to curb overseas investment thereby dramatically putting the finishing touch to a scenario that ensured the demise of manufacturing in the United Kingdom.

Industry was embarked upon a self-defeating cycle. Credit was taken from creditors and bank borrowings used as working capital but related as security to fixed assets. Working capital grew disproportionately to the growth in trade. Since, however, every concern was both creditor and debtor, the latter element in circulating capital grew disproportionately so that the flow of money fell to a mere trickle. At the same time, costs increased because of higher borrowings, prices had to be raised albeit belatedly, and demands for substantial wage settlements became automatic. Industry and commerce suffered a thrombosis from which they have never recovered.

The political platitude was to apply a tourniquet to stem the haemorrhage. This had the inevitable effect of cutting off the main hope of survival. Money had degenerated into a mass of clots injected into or abstracted from various parts of the anatomy. However efficient British Industry might have been on the factory floor, its financial mismanagement eliminated any hope of retention of the advantages gained as contributors to a famous victory in 1945. It almost deserved the appallingly inappropriate economic policy imposed upon it by consecutive governments.

Money, like blood, has two values.

First it is the infusion of life into an economic activity. Every businessman knows that there is no profit until he has money in the bank. A debt has not been settled until money has been received. Cash flow is the essence of business. Its control is the essential activity. Property, plant and machinery may represent success, but they may not be paid for. They can be monuments of achievement but are more likely to be epitaphs. Money needs no advertisement or publicity. If an entrepreneur makes money in the bank then he has made it.

All of which sounds simple enough. It goes without saying and being unremarked and unremarkable is often lost in the labyrinth of sophistication created by those who mistake education for experience. Nevertheless, it is a fundamental fact that for the body economic to grow, its circulation must be excellent. Blood transfusions are admissions of failure. Circulation is good only when all the members of the body are exercised and used for that which they were designed. That which controls the body must have confidence in its potential, an understanding of its capability as well as the desire for success. And so it is with the flow of money within and between the working parts of modern society. Where it is deemed to be more profitable to use money as an element of working capital, then that use will be preferred to any other and its rate of circulation will be consistently high. Alternative uses inevitably lead to transplants and temporary expedients.

The key to the velocity of money is therefore the confidence in the application of its use. Where it is believed that the application of working capital will generate high profits then money will be made to play its part. Discounts for prompt payment will be offered and taken. It is only the absence of confidence in achieve-ment that encourages an increase in volume and a reduction in velocity.

The second value of money is that it is ideal for use as a plasma. It can be abstracted from the body politic and bought and sold with relatively little risk. So, in times of uncertainty and high interest rates, the entrepreneur will favour the manipulation of a blood bank. Money once hoarded is seldom well spent. The confidence engendered by a substantial credit balance quickly transforms itself into an anxiety complex with almost a miserly attitude towards its maintenance and improvement. The relief from responsibility to a third party whose only interest literally is in the security charged to him and the ability to repay is so pleasurable as to create considerable reluctance and resistance towards a deliberate repetition of borrowing.

The true role of money within an economy is one of circulation. That role will be optimised when those who have the power to control its velocity are confident that the economy is capable of creating wealth.

International Use of Money

Each decade in this century has brought with it a unique combination of economic factors that has virtually eliminated any advantages from past experience and necessitated a constant return to basic studies of human behaviour. The 1980's is no exception and it has introduced a new medium of international exchange that has influenced an astounding number of factors which were previously considered sacrosanct and virtually untouchable. That medium is oil. As a result, the 1980's has witnessed the transformation of currency in the world market from a medium of exchange into a commodity. The generators of oil have succeeded the owners of gold, generators of gold having enjoyed but little significance as their production has been regarded as marginal in comparison with the value of stocks held around the world. But this is not so with oil. Production is deliberately equated to consumption and unused extracted stocks are insignificant compared with untapped resources under the control of the oil generators.

Unavoidable consumption of oil opened a floodgate of currency. The control of that currency was with sellers of oil for whom it was a replacement commodity. The immediate consequences were foreseen but not anticipated so that no avoiding action was taken.

One result so far has been that major currency values are no longer directly influenced by relative rates of interest, neither does adjustment to such rates have more than a marginal effect. A second is the emergence of international inflation and recession, a previously unknown phenomenon because of the stabilising influence of and the trust in gold. Substantial stocks of gold could only be accumulated over long periods of time and in the past the frequency of war was such that most hoards were depleted or replenished as the price of national survival and recovery.

Oil has introduced a new dimension into international media of exchange. Currencies have taken on the characteristics of commodities and have become vulnerable through inequality of distribution and control. A very small number of individuals can use the power that they have acquired through ownership of "hard" currencies to attack as commodities selected "soft" currencies for their profit. The sheer size of the blocks of major currencies that these entrepreneurs have at their command ensures a successful outcome for their sorties. Since there is virtually no defence to unexpected and infrequent attacks, their only limitation being avarice. Currency commodity trading has degenerated into a global game of poker whereat the richest will inevitably win. They have no bluff to be called.

An obvious strategy to combat the threat of currency manipulation in the future is to generate another medium of exchange which will also operate as a commodity. Western Nations have so far concentrated uopn the development of alternative energy resources if only to reduce their dependence upon oil. A more subtle and effective counter is that being adopted by the Japanese in preparing the way for substantial and influential overseas investments which will generate large earnings in the form of currencies under their influence and control.

But all is not gloom and despondency. The domination of international currencies by oil must be a temporary phenomenon.

Whilst in 1986 it might just be comparable to gold as a standard of measurement, it has one inherent weakness which will be its ultimate undoing. Unlike gold, oil is valued first by need and then by demand. The universal attraction of gold has been the consensus as to its value regardless of intrinsic need. The very strength of oil as a necessity allows it no defence other than economic need. Its value is sequential. Because it is physically in demand, it commands a price. Because the demand is great and international, the price has to be met with large amounts of international currency. Ownership of large volumes of one internationally recognised currency creates a unique power — but it is nevertheless shortlived.

The life-cycle of oil as the international currency dictator is in three phases. The first began when the implications of its economic potential were realised and acted upon. There is no doubt that historically oil had been under-priced, as indeed have been the natural resources of most countries that have had to rely upon others for their exploitation. The initial reaction was one of over-correction so that oil became considerably over-priced with the resultant international chaos. It over indulged its monopolistic position. The behaviour pattern was consistent with that of any commodity that suddenly appreciated its real worth. There was, however, one significant difference and that was the volume of world demand and its dependence on such a small number of supplies. The dramatic increase in price was reflected in an equally startling growth in the volume of U.S. dollars required to service an unchanged volume of business. The international currency market was thrown off balance and virtually out of control. The situation became so desperate that it could not continue and the cycle rapidly went into the second phase.

The physical demand for oil had to be stabilised so that price rises could be checked. Oil had reached a price level where world supplies could be increased by the introduction of economically marginal fields. It had become an exceedingly valuable commodity which justified exploration and investment. Circumstances differed as between established suppliers and the strength of oil's position depended upon unanimity amongst those who controlled its production. Suppliers jockeyed for advantage and users scrambled for economy. Within a comparatively short time, a mutually acceptable price plateau had been established and with it the crystallisation of the volume of U.S. dollars that would remain under the direct control of the oil sellers. For all practical purposes international trade was based on a standard, this time of oil, as against the past when it had been gold.

Yet even this phase is temporary. The third is just around the corner and whilst it must be a matter of conjecture, the essential elements already exist and the relevant behavioural pattern of the past in similar circumstances can be discerned. The physical need for oil must diminish, probably imperceptibly at first, then gradually accelerating as a result of a combination of a number of different factors. First, there will be a political will. Secondly there will be technological and environmental developments. Thirdly, economic alternatives will be promoted. As the need reduces, it is unlikely that production will fall so that price will become more competitive. When the trend becomes apparent, producer nations will break ranks and price will reduce sharply. The commodity will have followed the classical profile of a product life cycle. Coincidentally, as price and output fall, the disadvantages of a depreciating asset will be far less painful for nations such as the U.K. than had the reverse situation applied. As production and price of oil fall, the volume of U.S. dollars required to service the transactions will diminish very sharply. The point will be reached at which that amount of dollars will no longer be significant in terms of the total supply of currency necessary to support world trade. At that stage the rules for the determination of comparative rates of exchange will abruptly change. Oil will no longer dominate currencies and will be 'just another commodity'.

The next question to be asked is whether oil will be replaced by a similar commodity which in turn will dominate the money markets. The answer would appear to be no, despite the concentration by many nations upon energy conservation and food production, both of which have similar characteristics. The key to the success of oil as an international commodity currency was that the controllers of its supply were minute in number. There is no commodity visible at the present time which is so controlled.

In the absence of a unilateral standard of measurement, rates of exchange can only be determined by the relative significance of demand for the products and services of each country as well as the income due to it from its investments in other countries.

Those countries that have taken advantage of using the 'oil commodity' era to develop products and services for which there will be international demand, as well as to invest in other nations, will enjoy a considerable advantage over those who have not when comparative values are established.

As in all matters economic, accurate anticipation of change is the generator of future wealth. Realisation that a commodity dominated international currency market is but temporary does not reduce the burden of preparation but it does identify priorities and significance. The U.K. needs oil in the 1980's to defend itself. It must learn to avoid future dependence upon oil since one way or the other it is an asset that must depreciate. The United Kingdom must develop offensive economic weapons if, amongst other ambitions, it wishes to enjoy the future advantages of a strong international currency.

However traumatic the effect of oil may have been on the international money market, it has not permanently altered the basic human behaviour patterns of those responsible for lubricating world trade. But it has eliminated rules of the game that have been comfortably applied for many years although they were more suited to the times of their origin.

International currencies will retain the characteristics of commodities, but they will not depend upon use demand for the determintion of their value. Currency will be required as a means to an end and not as the consequence of a need.

The assumed correlation between baskets of similar goods in various parts of the world in order to arrive at basic rates of exchange is no longer tenable even in theory. Rates of exchange are no longer determined by comparative indigenous purchasing power. They may still determine the flow of business in the short term. For example, the tourist industry of one nation will benefit at the expense of another where current rates of exchange favour the purchasing power of the natives of the former nation, but this is a symptom and a result and no longer a cause. Over the longer period, it is doubtful whether fluctuation in currency values will be significantly affected by the flow of business. It is more likely that business will remain an opportunistic reaction rather than a remedy.

The temptation in the 1980's is for governments to embark upon national policies that are designed to control the internal distribution of a country's wealth amongst its inhabitants. They will succeed in much the same way and to the same extent as the management of a company that concentrate its energies on local markets, well established ranges and present competition. The policy is one of inetivable disaster. Either the management's inability to realise the potential of a company and the lack of provision for future growth results in the company being taken over by a more dynamic management from another company or it slides quietly away into voluntary liquidation. Governments that rely upon introvert policies, traditions and exhortation and ignore challenges outside their boundaries, do so at their peril. For certain, they will have little influence and no control over the international values attached to their currencies and they will ultimately be overwhelmed by those who pursue international strategies as priorities.

No government is an island and all are affected by the actions and reactions of those around them. The world is indeed a small place.

Time and decisions have been compressed into an explosive mixture that is far more volatile and powerful than any nuclear weapon.

The essential difference between foreign and domestic currency is that the first is primarily a commodity and the second is a medium of exchange. There is, however, one significant exception that proves the rule. Where a developed country lends money to a developing country it should do so in the form of working capital and not as a long term investment in bricks and mortar. The logic is quite clear. The developing country is determined to exploit its resources. Its economic attitude is identical to that of a small growing company. Opportunities are best exploited through expansion of marketing and distribution facilities. Profits are made through increased added value and not in fixed assets. Money invested in working capital will work. If its velocity is high, its effectiveness will be equally dramatic. A small amount will go a long way.

Unfortunately, but not surprisingly, the attitude of the developed countries towards their needy brethren is identical to that of the joint stock banks towards industry and commerce in the United Kingdom. Lenders look first for security, then towards reduction of exposure to risk, commercial rates of interest and side profits. Money is lent with ropes rather than strings and international loans often require the immediate use of the funds provided in the purchase of goods, etc. from nominated suppliers who are banker friendly. The balance sheets of developing countries become dominated by concrete yet their true value is in trade. Whilst the term "added value" is a superficial clarion call of the lenders, the investment is normally in infrastructure resources that by coincidence the lenders can provide. As a finishing touch, labour-saving machinery swamp over-populated societies.

The most effective helping hand does not conform to the rules of international banking which are simply a mirror image of those applied in domestic banking. Money should be invested where it will work. Velocity is more critical than volume. Every time money completes a cycle it can afford to pay interest. The longer the cycle, the less frequent the interest and the more likely it will be paid out of capital when the liability arises.

A further complication and equally understood as a banking protection is that repayment is inevitably in the form of an "international currency", i.e. one which has very little variance risk as far as the banker is concerned. It is potentially disastrous for a lender to insist upon capital and interest repayment in the form of, say, U.S. dollars, sterling or yen, unless the borrower's main market is the United States, Great Britain or Japan. Simply to provide the original loan in a major currency is not to ease the burden. It is often a device to ensure that the nominated suppliers obtain payment and that that part of the bargain is risk free for the lender.

Returning to basics, the purpose of the loan is to assist a nation to grow more rapidly and profitably than it otherwise would. This can only be brought about by an increase in the wealth of that country in a form for which there is a demand outside its boundaries. To use an external investment for the purpose of increasing internal wealth and then to require repayment in a stipulated international currency is a formula for wholesale bankruptcy. Ironically it is so far from economic reality that the lender is finally at the mercy of the borrower. The banker who lends money in amount and form inappropriate to its use will often find repayment unenforceable as insistance simply crystalises a loss.

Since 1945, international lending has incorporated all the destructive disincentives previously inherent in empire exploitation. So called developed countries have been very adept for centuries at plundering the natural resources of lands and people first as pirates and then as self-appointed guardians. Such a land might have produced a raw material that was highly regarded in

European markets. Those who represented the guardians would acquire the ownership of the acres capable of producing the desirable crop. Since the operational costs were minimal and those supervising the production were also small in number, shipment value of the crops was well below a price determined in normal competitive circumstances, particularly when the owners of the land were selling to related buyers and small margins kept the production supervisors personally in quite comfortable surroundings. But by far the greater proportion of added value was created in the country of refinement and consumption, that being the origin of the initial guardianship capital and the most comfortable place to enjoy the proceeds. Hence the multiplicity of huge family concerns which controlled all the salient parts of the economic equation to their benefit and the long term disadvantage of everyone else.

The final enforced relinquishment of empires eliminated this method of exploitation although the scars may well be a cause of irritation for many years to come. But the opportuniity still remains. There are still many countries that contain resources that titilate the palate of those who know how to use them. Guardianship has been replaced by international banking identical in philosophy and long term effect. Those countries that can still produce desirable raw materials but have neither the capital or the capitalistic competence, have been forced to seek the first and suffer the attentions of the second. The results are as disastrous economically as the original empiric approach. It is quite true that socially the effects appear to have been less damaging since the indigenous governments have used some of their borrowings to improve the lot of themselves and their people as necessary human and political gestures. The cost of the social investment has reduced the balance available for their economies, which has aggravated the economic problem. Whereas under the guardianship system some semblance of housing and education was sustained for the workforce and mutual benefit, in the mid-twentieth century the absence of good housekeeping has resulted in a greater imbalance between total investment and its return.

As a member of an empire, the developing country gained little from the extraction of its resources, was given little to re-invest and had no influence on the policy of exploitation or the methods employed. It had no idea as to the potential life-cycle for its resources in whatever form, where or what was its probable competition and what was needed to ensure a continuity of income beyond the immediate demand for its raw material. In every sense it was on a loser.

Under the present terms of international lending, a recipient of purchasing power abdicates its authority. The borrower is as firmly tied to the apron-strings of the lender as he ever was by the chains of colonialisation. The only advantage of being in debt is that if the debt is big enough the initiative may well pass from the lender to the borrower. Hence the present international situation. The terms of lending have been so far from the economic truth that they have proved to be self-defeating. The reason for such a rapid demise is because the policy was designed and implemented by bankers rather than entrepreneurs. Bankers are bankers the world over. The elimination of risk is not the elimination of profit. It is the destruction of capital. A small risk does not mean a small profit. It is more likely to result in no profit and some loss of capital. By definition, bankers have stocks of plasma. They are not physicians and even less do they comprehend the management of those who have actually benefited from the transfusion. They cannot be all things to all men and confine their expertise to an understanding of security, interest and repayment. But in international trade above all others, these three elements are but one leg of a three legged stool, and sitting on one leg is both painful and short-lived.

The first principle in international trade is that profit is enjoyed where it is earned. The price paid for a product or service at a point in a chain of sequential bargains is that which is competitive and determined by economic and not political reasons. If that price generates a profit which exceeds that which is needed to cover the cost and repayment of the related capital, then the surplus may be invested elsewhere. If, on the other hand, there is inadequate profit available in any segment of an economic process, then its continuity in its present form must be challenged. Transferring profit through pricing distorts international trade and will occasion erroneous investment criteria and inequitable taxation burdens. Profit which is not justifiably earned is inevitably wasted. It will encourage competition which may be misled, lead to complacency and ignore the necessity for technological improvement or innovation.

The second principle is that the intended use of finance determines the structure and terms of its provision. Use is therefore of the very considerable interest to both borrower and lender. The true burden and implications of its cost and repayment must be thought through by all concerned. If, for example, it is to be working capital then the characteristics of the loan must match those of working capital and not long term fixed assets.

The third principle is that the loan should be profitable to both parties. It is all too common to find hidden beneath the basic terms innumerable strings designed to be pulled and tightened as and when circumstances permit or opportunities arise. A mid-1980's U.K. analogy is that of a small company wishing to use the Unlisted Securities Market to raise finance finds that the cost of placing its shares can be engineered by its professional advisors to absorb almost half the proceeds of the placing. The true cost of borrowing should not be related to the bargaining power of the respective parties but to the potential exploitation of profits. Unless a developing nation does profit from its use of loans, it cannot borrow again. Even a golden egg is not worth the life of a goose if only because it may well lay others if encouraged to live and prosper. It is abundantly clear that the most vital element in any financial transaction is the viability and success of the borrower and yet this is too often sacrificed on the altars of security and interest.

There is a remarkable similarity between the responsibilities and conduct of the Board of Directors of an international conglomerate and the leadership of a nation which is much too close for comfort as far as the latter is concerned.

The shares of such a company are the equivalent to the currency of a nation. As far as the Board is concerned, they recognise that whilst in theory the value of their shares should represent the long term growth performance and prospects of their company, in practice share values can be greatly influenced by factors which are beyond their control. These might include technological developments in quite different industries, local politics and climatic conditions. Ignorance of their existence is no defence and failure to assess their implications is tantamount to suicide. Add to the equation the strategies of their competitors, and it becomes quite clear that the Board must apportion a very considerable amount of its time in making itself conversant with the company's total environment. It is the relationship between the company and its environment that will ultimately determine the value of its shares and indeed its continuity.

The nation's leaders have exactly the same task. Whatever the internal effectiveness of their currency, the external value attributed to it will be that determined by the relationship between their country's economy and that of the world as a whole. But equally important will be the fact that the assessment will not be made by them. It will be made by "the market" which will draw its own conclusions from what it sees from its view point. It will reflect to some extent its analysis of the effectiveness of the British government of the day but it will be more influenced by its impression of the long term potential that the nation can grasp.

The enigma is that no responsible director of an international conglomerate would accept his burden on the terms undertaken by the executive politician. The latter has neither the time or the incentive to devise an economic philosophy or an international strategy. In their absence it is quite unlikely that the United Kingdom will do other than react to external developments as in the past, so that in the future its external currency management will continue to stagger from one crisis to another and its internal monetary control dribble and stutter.

Inflation

Inflation is the curse of growth and the harbinger of change. Since the advent of the Industrial Revolution, the politician has lashed his electorate with the scourge of modern economics, Inflation. In its early days Inflation was but one of the nine tails. By 1970 it had grown into a monstrous deterrent, a punishment to be avoided at all costs. Society could be sacrificed on the altar of its appeasement and no strain was too great in the achievement of its control. Inflation was the bête noir of the British economy and the beat of the drum in the bowels of the long boat. It will be very difficult for the economists of the future to understand the over-emphasis of a problem that had been given the magnitude of incurable cancer unless they examine objectively the motivation and ambitions of politicians at the time. The division of the economy into classes enabled the politician to divide and rule. The concentration upon the terrors of Inflation allowed the politician to add a dimension as well as a demarcation. Labour costs were deemed by one party to be the root cause of the dreaded disease, whilst the other party ignored that argument and concentrated upon the increased prices imposed by the get-rich-quick and profit hungry minority. Each party sought to make its point and neither moved towards the other. Unfortunately for those they governed, the truth of the economic matter provided no political advantage. Indeed, it would have obviated most of the causes of social discontent and politicians would have been hard put to justify their existence.

So what is the secret of Inflation that has been so carefully ignored? The answer lies in the study of the relationship between the cost of labour and the added value attributed to its use, a study which has shown that for almost a century that relationship has remained remarkably constant.

The total equation is quite straight forward. Selling price less the cost of material and service inputs equals the added value. Added value is the cost of labour, plus the profit, which includes capital return and payment.

At first sight it would seem quite inconceivable that throughout a century of many revolutionary processes and technological innovations the relationship between added value and the cost of labour could remain constant. A more natural result should be that the labour content would diminish, yet that has not happened. The reasons may be quite simple.

The constant factor in the equation has been man. His ego has not changed. He is the arbiter of value. He decides his preferences and these in broad terms have remained consistent. As man has progressed through survival and necessity towards luxury, his views as to the relative importance of material things have not changed. The luxuries of today become the necessities of tomorrow. High prices will always be offered for ego satisfaction. Man himself sets the standard and thereby pre-determines the outcome. The constant thread throughout his economic activity has been, and remains, his concept of preference.

The second reason is that despite political interference, man has increased the effectiveness of his application so that as his wage packet has increased so has his productive performance. He receives more purchasing power now than he did a century ago. He also contributes more value to the nation's wealth. It demonstrates a basic pattern of human behaviour unaffected in the long term by political expediences.

Acceptance that there is indeed a constant relationship between labour cost and added value is a very significant step towards the understanding of the cause of inflation. Armed with that we can forecast and prepare for the social consequences. We still cannot hope to be able to control fully but we can alleviate the inevitable.

Let us start first with the political definition of inflation. This is that the rate of inflation is the rate of increase in retail prices. It is confined to the pound in your pocket (despite political assertions to the contrary illustrating the consistency of political advice) and assumes that the electorate is concerned primarily with supermarkets, building societies and holidays. It is a simple measurement, readily understood, easily obtained and as easily manipulated. It is an ideal statistic, but for all the concentration given to it, it is still but the tip of an enormous iceberg. Above the surface, it is a warning to shipping. Yet it provides no clue to its true size, shape or history beneath the surface. Concentration upon price as the true indicator of inflation has led the politician inexorably back to a comparison between two absolutes based on the sole relativity of time. In truth, the measurement is relative but not in time which is only one component part. The critical relationship is between wages and added value. Price is a contributory factor to both. Price is the result of a decision. It is the outcome of an attempt at balance between assumed external pressures and assessed internal factors. It is an expression of calculated hope. Prices are fixed in the hope that sales and profit will result. Prices are maintained whilst losses are not incurred and sales are sustained.

Perhaps the most important characteristic is that price is a mixture of historic intelligence and future assumptions. The timing of price movements is more critical than their significance.

During the 1970's a method of governmental control was introduced whereby industry had to obtain permission before it could increase its prices. The object was to slow down the rate of inflation by putting a brake, albeit mainly through administrative procedures, on the upward spiral of prices. Increases had to be justified. At first, industry regarded the imposition with fear and anger. But they complied. The effect of the discipline which thereafter had to be observed was that for the first time in many of the older established industries in the United Kingdom, price increases were recommended before the effect of the cause of the increase had begun to bite. For the very first time, increases in costs were anticipated. It also had the effect of eliminating the "wait and see what our competitors do first" adage. Finally, it shifted the emphasis from sales volume to profitability. Salesmen were no longer allowed to insist that prices had to be maintained otherwise business would be lost.

As with almost every quasi-economic decision imposed for political purposes, price control achieved a quite unforeseen result. It concentrated management's attention on price policies which preceded necessity. An outstanding example of this was the iron foundry industry. For decades, the time lag between increases in costs and price rises had been such that the industry had always struggled to make profits commensurate with the investment needed to keep the foundries up-dated. For decades, the industry had constructed its costs on a logic that was consistent with the nineteenth century, with the result that customers had enjoyed whole ranges of castings at prices well below their economic cost. Unfortunately, the Foundry Price Commission was far too late to do other than delay the inevitable decimation of an industry so misled and mismanaged. Nevertheless, the lesson remains for all to see. Prices are indeed critical, but it is the chain of facts, logic and assumptions leading to their definition, that controls an economy. Time is the essence of Pricing policy.

The principles are abundantly clear. The entrepreneur cannot accept a loss and the market will refuse at too high a price. Each must try alternative sources of satisfaction. Before examining the implications of the two statements, it is worthwhile to pause and consider the true sensitivity of price. It is in fact extremely difficult to establish the ceiling in terms of price for any given product. Certainly in the short and medium term, customers will accept quite substantial increases if only through inertia or immediate lack of alternatives. Many businesses have been saved from disaster by a ruthless upwards review of prices on the principle that unacceptance is no more painful than selling at a loss. In a large number of instances quite considerable price rises have been accepted with very little demur and remained thereafter as established plateaux. The overriding consideration is normally that of value for money and in the case of many products and services that includes consistency of quality in all its aspects. It is true to say that in the modern market place most products command a monopolistic position if only through extensive advertising. A loss of market share is seldom brought about through considered price increases.

In many established British industries prices were held down far too long and their competitive levels obscured the cost of poor service and quality. Too often orders were forthcoming initially through pre-1939 reputation and then through a combination of lack of investment and progress in design, the costs of which were avoided thereby assisting the maintenance of low prices. At the same time, wages remained low so that there appeared to be a balance between purchasing power and stable prices. The problem was that equilibrium had been achieved at the wrong levels and there was no margin in the system to prepare for the return of international competition. When necessity arrived, prices could be and were dramatically increased, but the lack of investment and foresight took their toll. There was no margin in quality and service that could compensate for higher prices. British exports lived or died on price. In many industries demise was inevitable.

The apparent correlation between prices and wages proved irresistible. Even the Bank of England supported the view that control of the latter automatically led to the control of the former. The attitude of the politician in not wishing to make it clear that he has really no influence on the economics of business other than to increase its costs can readily be understood. That of the establishment was less obvious. Perhaps they were more swayed by the political winds than they would otherwise admit. Whatever their motivation, politicians and bankers jumped into the fray with great abandonment. The United Kingdom was set on a course from which none of them wished to deviate, the battle of the wages.

For a short period, the general theory appeared to be correct. During the early 1980's, inflation dropped dramatically. Wage increases appeared to be minimal although unemployment rose to record levels. But the respite was short and coincided with enormous social and community problems. One swallow did not make a summer. The truth was that wages were not, and had never been, the root cause of inflation. The answer is to be found elsewhere and is politically unpalatable.

Added value determines the reward of labour and capital. Added value can only be determined after setting a price and deducting therefrom the cost of material and services. The final price is in theory adjusted by the market. In the first instance, however, the decision-maker is influenced almost exclusively by the cost of material and services. These he has to recover for certain. These he himself has little chance of influencing. He has to ensure continuity and availability. The time cycle between ordering his input and receiving payment for his output may be extremely long and even span several years. He may be involved in foreign currency. The implications are obvious. Material has overtaken labour as the key cost of production. Perhaps a hundred years ago when the skilled craftsman reigned supreme his availability and wage rates were the elements upon which the entrepreneur based his plans, but not so post-1970. The investment cycle in the methods of the application of labour, such as plant automation, allow business to spread the labour costs involved over a number of years. Materials and services permit no respite.

But what, in real terms, is Inflation? It is a state of imbalance between the costs of material and service inputs and added value caused by an increase in selling price, when price has been increased beyond that which was necessary to maintain the previous equilibrium or when selling price remains constant but material and service input costs fall. The alternative, i.e. that material and service input costs rise but selling price remains constant so that price is insufficient to sutain the previous added value creates a state of deflation. Since there are always delays in every market place, actual costs are seldom related to actual prices. Prices are very occasionally anticipatory but usually reactionary. An improvement in intelligence will encourage anticipation, as we have seen, intervention will also lead to anticipation. It follows therefore that in a modern developed society there will normally be a constant imbalance and periods of inflation and deflation.

The first reaction to this theory is that a comprehensive intelligence system permits control of effect. If the key factor which triggers off price rises is the cost of material and services input, then the extent to which fluctuations in these costs can be accurately forecast will determine the sensitivity potential of price increases.

If this theory is correct then the present political definition of a state of inflation may be quite wrong both as to timing and consequences and that can be illustrated as follows. If we start in a state of equilibrium then a series of movements in the cost of input with a delayed reaction as to price can result in periods of time during which the definition of state, i.e. inflation or deflation or stability, will be different according to the method of assessment, political or economic.

Thus, where the input costs have risen with no price increase, the political definition is one of stability. The economic definition is deflation. Then when input costs continue to rise and there is an inadequate increase, but nevertheless an increase in prices, the economist will maintain that there is still a state of deflation, whilst the politician will shout "inflation". Further price increases may result in a period where politician and economist agree that they have lift off, i.e. inflation. But the sequence soon divides. When input costs level off, the economist will change his tune more quickly than the politician and recognise stability before the latter. Then when the costs of input fall, but prices remain constant, the politician will observe stability and the economist a return to inflation. The final stage for our purpose is that prices then fall slightly, leaving the politician happily chanting deflation but the economist still gloomily muttering inflation. Unfortunately for the populace, the economist is nearer the truth and their reaction to his interpretations would be more effective at least in smoothing the uncertainties of forward decisions. The politician is concentrating upon the reaction of the market, rather than the root cause.

But is it enough to dismiss labour entirely from the problem by the acceptance of a constant relationship between the cost of labour and the added value of which it is a part? The politician wil undoubtedly, as indeed he must, insist that labour cost increases will upset the equilibrium and therefore have the same effect outlined above as the movements in the cost of inputs other than labour. The immediate reaction to an increase in wages is to increase the added value by raising prices. It is quite true that politically we then have inflation, prices have risen. But, and it is a most important but, if the absolute increase in price equals the total increase in added value the constituent parts retaining their relative values, balance is sustained. Labour and capital have increased their reward in the same proportion. Both can afford the new price level. The purchasing power of their money has remained constant. Economically there is no inflation.

The qualities of labour set it apart from all other resources. Its measurement as to cost is quickly and easily calculated. In most circumstances it can be predetermined as the production cycle is long enough for price response to coincide with increases in labour costs. It has no currency problems. It is not subject to as many uncontrollable factors as, for example, imported materials.

Therefore for all its well-publicised disadvantages, labour is the most certain element of cost.

Let us next assume that for whatever reason prices cannot be adjusted to absorb all the increase in labour costs. Do we then have inflation? Politically yes, simply because there has been an increase in prices. But economically we have a far more dangerous situation, namely deflation. By assumption, the cost of material services input has remained constant. Therefore the sufferer can be only the portion of the added value other than labour costs, i.e.

capital return and repayment. This reduction in reward discourages further investment, yet the apparent cost of labour relative to profit signals a reduction needed in labour cost. The absence of reasonable profits means an inability to pay for investment which is further exacerbated by the rise in prices. That which is taken to be inflation is in fact the cause of more economic ills than that which is truly inflation for the simple reason that the inaccurate interpretation leads to a response exactly opposite to that which is really required.

Inflation is the state of imbalance between the constituent parts of added value, namely the rewards attributed to labour and capital, brought about by the inefficiency of the price mechanism to respond to increases in the cost of material/service input.

Deflation is the state of imbalance arising from the inadequate price adjustment needed to respond to input cost decreases.

The increases/decreases in material/service inputs are imposed, unavoidable and uncontrollable. In the short term they must be paid for. Substitution at a later date may be practicable and acceptable, in which event some control may then be exerciseable.

Timing is the key factor in the attempt to control inflation. In theory it should be possible to anticipate the ultimate effect of imposed cost increases. In practice, there are many impediments, few of which have so far been overcome.

The causes of lack of response include a lack of intelligence (related information), failure of communication, lack of reaction, comprehension, knowledge data and planning, plus deliberate intervention for political and human reasons, the latter being well justified. In the human environment within its palisade of imaginary security there is every incentive to resist change. That which approaches outside the defences is repulsed at the last ditch and never met half way. Suggestions of change from within have few supporters and many antagonists. Since the essence of response is the recognition of necessity before inevitability, it is extremely unlikely that any democratic society will be prepared to accept the discomfort of self-imposed change and therefore the rigours of anticipatory measures. Inflation and deflation will continue virtually unchecked.

In addition to the fear of change, man will always prefer to make no decision rather than choose. He will fail to observe that to be indecisive is to decide to defer, a decision in itself. He believes that the absence of a positive decision avoids future responsibility, whereas the responsibility for omission is as great as that of commission. He seeks comfort in the assertion of "not me, sir", failing to observe the grave responsibility for abdication.

Of all men, the politician is the most fearful of change. That imposed from without can be explained as inevitable and uncontrollable. But that which is proposed from within will only be eagerly grasped by opponents who will seek to comfort the masses by insisting that change is unnecessary and they need not be disturbed. Since the politician who tells those about him that which they want to hear is the one who is accorded the vote, the risk of declaiming change by self-imposition is tantamount to political suicide.

Add to that factor the peculiar aspects of inflation and the course of the politician allows no deviation. The two significant elements in inflation according to the politician are wages and prices. The former denotes labour and the latter capital. Whether he is red or blue, the temptation is irresistible. The socialist will defend the wage increase as a human right. The conservative will attack the wage increase as a selfish and irresponsible approach to the problem. Socialists will endeavour to control price rises which they depict as merely a means to increase undeserved profits. Conservatives will overtly and covertly control wages by public sector domination and government support in wage bargaining. Inflation is a political dream.

The statistics are simple — but meaningless. The subject is simple to explain — but in actuality grossly complex. Above all the battleground is clearly defined and nicely positioned. Inflation becomes a human nightmare.

And yet, Inflation is only a disease when an otherwise natural state of being is incorrectly depicted and remedies applied that seek to achieve political results through aggravation. The continuous application of dirt to an itch must lead eventually to an infected wound and even to amputation.

The politician will defend his position by the argument that failure to look after a minor complaint can lead to a dreaded disease. So he will warn "beware of the roaring inflation" carefully avoiding the fact that the self-appointed physician creates the very epidemic that he now wishes to avoid. His remedies aggravate and inflame. The germ is allowed to blossom unheeded and ignored simply because the physician will not admit he neither understands nor wishes to understand the true cause of the complaint.

In other than the most exceptional circumstances, Inflation is a normal desirable state of affairs enabling an economy to grow and entrepreneurs to take reasonable risks. Surges in the rate of inflation correctly defined represent imbalances caused by events or factors beyond the control or influence of any one economy. Such surges can be forecast and to some extent alleviated as to ultimate effect. Repetition can be avoided by accurate forecasting and preparation for substitution. The first earthquake will cause havoc. The second in the same place is as destructive as the populace are incompetent in their preparations for its resistance.

Risk equals profit. Without one, the other cannot be achieved, as profit without risk attracts a multiplicity of competition. Profit serves two masters, he who provided the original capital and he who used the capital to create the profit. They may be one and the same. Nevertheless there are two distinct roles and each expects its reward. So risk has to equal an acceptable return on capital invested including compensation for effort and expertise. Also included in the return on capital invested is an element of capital repayment. Capital requires a return and to be returned. The original investment was a finite sum of currency and the obligation to repay is satisfied when that finite sum is handed back, either over a period or at its termination. The value of the sum will depend on its purchasing power when it is repaid. If, during the period of its loan, the value of money has decreased, then the burden of repayment is alleviated. The value of relief is that attributed to the cost of inflation.

The advantage in devaluation of currency holds good notwith-standing the attendant disadvantages arising from the impact of Inflation on the day to day management of the entrepreneur and the problems caused by increasing costs and prices. It is significant enough to encourage entrepreneurs to assume long-term burdens which in the absence of Inflation could be disastrous. Without Inflation and in a democratic society influenced by quasi-social conscience the entrepreneur is on a hiding to nothing.

The benefits from Inflation extend beyond the employer and capitalist. Whatever the statistical assessment of today's costs and prices, it cannot be denied that over many decades the average level of the standard of living has improved at a rate which would have been considered impossible a hundred years ago. There have been many reasons for this change, the more influential being technological innovation, mass production and marketing and variances in relative price changes for whatever reasons.

Inflation encourages periods of investment which ultimately bear fruit in the improvement of the economic use of resources. Without Inflation there can be no significant growth in absolute or relative terms.

What is an acceptable rate of Inflation where the rate is defined as at present, i.e. the rate of reduction in the purchasing power of money? This is the key question that any politician seeks to avoid other than in the most general terms. He knows that any precise annual rate that he may select can be compounded over a number of years into an awe-inspiring statistic. The attractive value of statistics to a nimble-minded politician is in their use as incontravertible, unsupportable and totally misleading defensive data.

The fact of the matter is that the measurement of acceptability is again one of relationship and cannot be absolute. It is not just "single figures" or a nice round "5 per cent" or a minimum rate of "1 per cent". An acceptable rate of inflation is the minimum that will encourage investment thereby maintaining the growth of an economy and improvement in its standard of living. That rate is where the cost of borrowing equates the rate of price increase.

The entrepreneur must earn sufficient to pay for the actual cost of his borrowings and also accumulate a fund equal to the capital loan for its ultimate repayment. The greater the cost of borrowing, the higher the selling price needed to maintain the fund creation. The higher the price, the greater the sales resistance and the more likely the increase in labour costs. A high cost of borrowing therefore necessitates a high rate of inflation.

Conversely a low rate of interest will lead to selling price stability and a low rate of inflation. At first sight, this appears to be an ideal combination. In fact, however, the stability of prices reduces the long-term gain otherwise derived from the depreciation in the value of money and the corresponding reduction in the true cost of capital repayment.

It follows, therefore, that where market conditions permit, the ideal rate of inflation is that which equates the net cost of borrowing. The entrepreneur can then regard the negative cost of borrowing as being offset by the positive gain in the reduction of

85

the true cost of capital repayment. He can then identify with some certainty the profit that he can enjoy during the lifetime of the investment. The balance between the cost of borrowing represented by the rate of inflation is a nice one. The entrepreneur has a preference towards the latter. He will be more encouraged to borrow money if he believes that its ultimate repayment will be substantially eased by the passage of time and the erosion through inflation. This preference is further accentuated by the impact of taxation on the current cost of borrowing. The equation becomes complicated by the fact that taxation is a cost and must be reflected in both selling price and devaluation of money. As far as the entrepreneur is concerned, therefore, it alleviates the net cost of borrowing. He will be most encouraged to invest during periods of high taxation, increased selling prices and an increased rate in devaluation of money. Whilst in the short term the burden of taxation is a contributor to instability it is not of itself a deterrent to the entrepreneur when he plans his investments. It may well be that the impact of taxation leading to political inflation will encourage investment on the grounds that the ultimate real profit will be derived from the devaluation of the money and therefore the cost of its repayment.

The promise of a zero rate of inflation is a tempting political objective. It can be presented as the acme of economic efficiency. The value of money is presumed to remain constant so that wage increases can be confined to those that adequately represent improvements in productivity.

In fact, it is an impossible scenario. No country can determine a zero rate of inflation for itself. It cannot control the cost of its imported raw materials, goods or services. It cannot fix unilaterally an internationally acceptable rate of exchange for its own currency. During the 1980's and probably the 1990's also, the best that any single government can inspire to achieve is to minimise its internal rate of inflation to as close to the absolute minimum set by international external influences and forces as it can.

Even if it were possible, is a zero rate of inflation economically desirable? The answer must be No for a number of reasons.

First there is the cost of capital repayment and the inherent incentive for entrepreneurial exploitation as explained earlier.

Secondly, an economy needs to grow absolutely and relatively. Absolute growth is a function of inflation.

Thirdly, a zero rate of interest is commercially unacceptable unless there is a negative rate of inflation. Such a combination would create an imbalance that would be uncontrollable and could not continue for any length of time without damaging the economy.

Fourthly, a world-wide zero rate of inflation would be even more disastrous than the present situation in international investment for the developing countries.

Finally, it would dramatically change the basic structure of capital investment eliminating long term fixed securities, reducing short term loans and concentrating capital resources in the various forms of equity. Its continuance would take economists into completely unknown country, create a host of absolutely new problems and unforeseeable and previously unacceptable combinations of factors which would have far-reaching political implications.

Whilst a zero rate of inflation remains a point on a graph through which the actual rate may very occasionally and very temporarily pass, past experience and common sense can prevail and a reasonable state of economic equilibrium can be sustained. But in no circumstances within the present state of the art and science of economics in politics can such a rate be an ultimate desirable target.

Unemployment

Unemployment as presently defined is unavoidable because the creative capacity of and the effort of application by man in the use of his resources exceeds his capacity to consume. As man becomes more ingenious in 'work-saving' technology, the constant input of time allocated to his economic activity will result in an ever increasing output to the point where inevitably he is producing a physical surplus. His only course in a competitive environment is to reduce his time input. The total number of hours of 'work' available in an economy will exceed the number required to provide the goods and services for which there is a demand. The margin between the two, i.e. unwanted available hours, represents the unavoidable unemployment. The outcome is further exacerbated by the immobility of labour, the regional differences between supply and demand for labour and the incompatibility between skills needed and those offered.

Man has failed to pre-empt the inevitable because:

1. He dislikes the discomfort of self-imposed change.
2. He prefers short term profit.
3. He prefers popularity.
4. He can leave the problem to others.

The significant causes of unemployment are:

1. The historic development of industry and commerce.
2. The speed of technological revolution.
3. Political intervention and disturbance.

Developed countries are the grave-yards of numerous industries. The landscape is cluttered with disused mines, rusty skeletons of shipyards, raised factories and collapsed chimneys. Industries have come and gone but during their lifetime it would have been considered sacrilege even to suggest that their existence might prove finite.

The repetitive pattern is clearly defined. Innovation attracts demand. Its satisfaction is most efficiently achieved by locating the applicants of the necessary resources in an area where advantages can be gained simply by geographical concentration. These might range from raw materials through transport facilities to skilled labour. Once one company has established itself and has obviously profitted from its physical situation, other entrepreneurs become attracted to that particular area like bees to the honey-pot. The industry itself is established and crystalised. All remains well until the unthinkable happens; it declines and falls. As demand diminishes, for whatever reasons, surplus resources begin to emerge in that area and those resources include labour. Buildings can be re-used, land can be reclaimed and machinery can be scrapped, but people cannot be destroyed; they remain immobile and become very voluble. It is no surprise that politicians postpone the problem as long as they possibly can and then side-step it when it can no longer be ignored. Yet if the cycle is inevitable and the decline with all its consequences unavoidable, the question is why cannot it be forestalled? The answer lies in the fact that the present preferred control structure embraced by developed societies in the Western hemisphere is one of political democracy and in that potential leaders cannot survive unless they all apply the same rules of the game. It would be considered suicidal for one political leader alone to tell the truth as he saw it and to initiate counter-measures that were unpalatable and uncomfortable thereby allowing other political leaders to take advantage of the unpopularity of such measures to propagate the policy that either the forecasts were unnecessarily pessimistic or that the anticipated problems could be resolved without discomfort.

The problem is further compounded by the fact that since industry organised itself regionally, unemployment becomes a localised malaise. It can be isolated and rendered less effective in national political terms. Deep depression scattered amongst the electorate can develop into black holes without dramatically affecting the national vote. Industry has played into the hands of the politician. The economic advantages it has enjoyed through regional development enhance local unemployment problems. Their impact on national politics is limited with the majority in numbers of constituencies relatively unaffected.

There is, however, a secondary difficulty which reflects human nature. Those who enjoy the fruits of success are the last to admit that their enjoyment will be temporary. The longer the established way of life and the more comfortable the existence, the greater the disinclination of those who lead to acknowledge any other future than that of continuity. The country-side is lettered with gravestones inscribed with the tragic words 'if only'.

Unemployment is an inevitable reflection of economic life. It can be clearly defined both as to when and how much in exactly the same way as any other input resource. The reason why it's related social problem has not been resolved is because the democratic system is not conductive to the integrity of leadership. Democracy panders to human nature and therefore shuns, ignores or deliberately disbelieves any adverse prognostication. Even when it becomes acutely visible and embarrassingly unavoidable, un-employment being regional in effect has little direct influence in political terms upon those who depend upon a national majority to retain power. However large their number, the unemployed cannot directly bring down a government.

In any event, politicians who forecast doom and gloom risk their livelihood. Even the most outspoken British politician when asked in 1985 to confirm whether a particular industry was well equipped for the future could only respond that to the best of his knowledge and belief 'its current capacity equated the current demand.' As for the managers of industry, those who make cautionary comment are rejected as defeatists and purveyors of excuses.

People constitute a peculiar resource, not only because of social and religious considerations but because they, uniquely amongst all resources, can have a profound effect upon their political leaders. But in all other features, labour as an economic resource is no different to its fellows in the production of wealth. The causes for its non-use are common to all resources and can be readily identified. Whilst there is confusion and conflict in the resolution of the problem of surplus labour, there need be no confusion or misunderstanding concerning the reason why it exists.

The deaf and blind approach, adopted in the past towards the inevitable, exemplifies the vanity and insecurity of man. Since these are characteristics which cannot be erased, the pattern of behaviour is indelible and repetitive. Even in the mid 1980's the

United Kingdom has the foundations and dampcourses of future ruins in the form of the high rise office blocks, silicone valleys and small unit factory estates.

The only acceptable solution to unemployment in countries which pride themselves on their democratic mode of government is that of setting aside resources to alleviate the discomfort of being out of work and hoping that the cost can be covered by the wealth generated by those remaining economic occupations. The equation is continuously balanced by extracting from it surplus resources which equate the marginal excess supply of labour. Any attempt to reallocate resources in anticipation of a change in either the volume or character of demand is politically impossible. In the past this has only been achieved where there has been the threat of aggression or actual warfare.

This assessment should not be regarded as defeatist. That unemployment cannot be resolved in the short term for the reasons given above is a fact. Politicians will vie with each other to deny such a conclusion since they will, whatever their colour, wish to hold out the carrot of its resolution. It would be as equally dangerous for them to admit that it cannot be resolved as to prophesy its emergence.

Unemployment is one of the costs of democracy. The best that can be hoped for is that government will have a capability to forecast its timing and extent and then to make provision for its cost. To expect any government to implement preventative action is to ask the impossible.

The economic consequences and implications of unemployment within the parameters as set out above can be clearly stated.

When unemployment rises and those remaining in work receive a total reward of the same magnitude as that previously received by the total labour force and the added value of wealth created in a nation remains constant, then the increased costs of unemployment reduce either the proportion of added value attributable to government or the proportion available for capital payment and return, or a combination of both.

Where, however, unemployment rises but national added value also increases whilst total inputs remain constant then the initiative is with the government to acquire the marginal increase in added value and use it to cover the cost of the increased unemployment.

On the assumption that unemployment is unavoidable then the

most acceptable economic policy for the United Kingdom is to create additional added value, maintain the total reward payable to labour and in so doing increase their per capita income. The government can then take the appropriate action to ensure that the marginal increase in added value comes under its control and direction and is not absorbed as increased return on capital and the facility to repay capital.

Statistical Misrepresentation

Unemployment statistics are the playing fields of the politician and civil servant. The politician determines the rules for classification and collection in the hope, common to all parties, that the resultant presentation will minimise any insoluble problems. The civil servant exercises his considerable mathematical muscle to do his best to embarrass his current masters. It is a matching of wits and a game of chance — for all except the unfortunates whom the statistics purport to represent.

Since it is now the age of the computer, the overwhelming desire is to regurgitate the same information for as many different purposes as possible rather than examine too closely the appropriate nature or even the validity of the basic data that has been collected. Thus, in the United States unemployment figures are obtained by statistical sampling, a branch of the tree of knowledge carefully nurtured by those who sell the output of public opinion polls whose reputation hardly encourages a wider application of their art.

In the United Kingdom, because the payment of government money far outweighs all other aspects of economic activity in its national importance, it is natural for those who make such a judgement to turn to the data that identifies the fortunate recipients. Since the prime qualification required of certain beneficiaries is that they are out of work, it is logical to use their numbers as being those unemployed. It is argued that there can be no doubt as to the accuracy of that data, and the costs of collection, collation and presentation are for all practical purposes already covered. The small matter that such a definition is by no means comprehensive is dismissed as being of less importance than that of accuracy. The more significant aspect of the definition of accuracy is ignored completely. After all the trend is the thing and on this matter the ball can be passed backwards and forwards with great abandon. Trends necessitate complex adjustments for seasonal variations, external factors and all sorts of mental gymnastics.

Obscurity can be guaranteed so that opposing politicians can equal 'disappointing' with 'disastrous', 'improving' with 'little change' and 'encouraging' with 'calamitous'. No politician wants to acknowledge publicly the absolute truth for fear of ultimate responsibility for problem creation or resolution.

In certain European democracies, West Germany and Switzerland being the outstanding examples, unemployment figures are clouded by the inclusion of foreign workers who can be imported or exported at comfortable notice. Unlike their British counterparts, immigrant labour enjoys no security of tenure in either West Germany or Switzerland. Their title is a work permit which is exactly that and no more. Citizenship whether by right or application is quite a different matter. Since they are what they are immigrant workers are ideal subjects for statistical analysis and manipulation. The advantage is not lost upon their political hosts.

Regardless of country, the combination of politician and civil servant welded together in statistical harmony is an unholy alliance designed to persuade the ignorant populace that the current facts support that which they want to hear. The politician decides on the latter. The civil servant provides the former. The facts are statistics — and everyone knows what they are . . . caveat emptor.

Philosophical

What is unemployment? Why do politicians avoid its definition? Perhaps the answer is in the rising sun and casting light might just be detrimental to those who seek to divide and rule.

Whichever way the figures are presented and regardless of their presenter, there would appear to be very little unemployment in Japan as defined in the West. Even in the 1980's a Japanese employee stays with one employer during his working life. It would appear that loyalty is repaid by security. On closer examination, however, it is not that simple. An essential feature of the bargain is the level of wages. A more vital feature is the continuity of payment of wages and that is the heart of the matter. In Japan, to be unemployed is simply to say that one is not in receipt of wages. If wages are paid regardless of effort then the recipient is employed. The fact that he simply 'clocks on and off' is neither immoral nor dishonest.

As far as the Japanese are concerned the argument is quite clear. An offer of employment is an offer of income. The acceptance of that income requires an offer of effort and application. The provision of work is entirely the responsibility of the employer who accepts the burden knowing that at some future date it may well become a liability in that he may not be able to keep the employee fully occupied. Nevertheless he will still have to pay his wages. There is no direct relationship between current effort and current reward. That is a western approach, and the desire to equate wages to current achievement has proved the undoing of western economies. The argument that it must be morally right that a man should be paid precisely what he is worth whilst he is at work would appear to be quite overwhelming, but it assumes that work will always be available. That we now know cannot be so. The improvement in the utilisation of resources over the last two centuries will ultimately create a constant excess of capacity to supply over capacity to consume even where the former involves directly the application of human labour.

The basic equation is the balance between he who offers his labour and he who offers to use it. The mutual commitment is reflected in the monetary terms. Unfortunately, such a simple approach smells of servility or even slavery, both emotive and politically attractive subjects which have long been discarded, at least theoretically, as unworthy and inhuman.

It has therefore been an easy task for those who curry popular favour to persuade all shades of votes that the only right approach is to pay a man what he is truly worth, however impracticable or shortsighted that may be.

Work is an ethos that has been promoted to an ethic. Unemployment has degenerated from loss of face and income into a sin. Work has become a 'right' which is economic nonsense simply because the retention of that right necessarily means the retention of specific jobs, methods and processes which have deteriorating added value for many reasons. "Right" implies a one way traffic regardless of any other considerations. In fact, the activity applying the capability of man is an obligation which is mutual and therefore equitable. The obligation may be between State and the individual or between corporate or private entity and an individual. In either case, it is entered into freely and with comprehension of its implication.

In the Western hemisphere, society is facing the problem of occupation, i.e. how the populace can occupy itself, if only to keep it out of mischief. In essence, the problem is not economically insoluble since science and technology have made it possible for society as a whole to retain an acceptable standard of living and support financially those who are unable to contribute towards it. The social problems are immense and are the inevitable consequences of a short term exploitation by the power seekers and their propaganda.

The clock cannot be turned back, neither can the education of the past be unlearnt. There is no dramatic solution to unemployment but there is the practicable possibility of easing its future impact. That can only be achieved by a change in philosophy made possible by understanding and integrity.

It is far better for all concerned if a man is paid for his potential contribution throughout the time he wishes to work and that in return for that willingness, an employer should undertake the responsibilities of providing reasonable payment and opportunity for the man to apply his capabilities. If the employee is mis-trained so that his skills become irrelevant, then his employer is the loser and is encouraged either to avoid that error or quickly to rectify it. If the employee wishes to raise his income then he is encouraged to suggest ways and means whereby added value can be increased, or accept greater responsibility.

The vital factor is the rate of reward. Labour is regarded no longer as a Profit and Loss debit. It is an investment on the Balance Sheet. When a company buys a sophisticated expensive machine, the justification is that its output will earn in the years ahead more than sufficient to cover its cost. That the decision will be economically justified. The management accept the responsibility for finding the work load, obtaining orders and financing its use. It is suggested that during the last quarter of the twentieth century and into the foreseeable future, the application of labour and technology will be viewed economically and socially in exactly the same light. Taking on employees offers the same opportunities and incurs the same responsibilities as any other investment in production capacity. Men are Balance Sheet figures.

The implications, however, range far beyond the employer/employee relationship. The philosophy suggested would lead to the elimination of Trade Union involvement as defined in 1985 and the elevation of that body into the political arena proper. Wage rates would relate to the national standard of living and the balance between the numbers at any one time productively employed and those not so employed. The added value concept would be vital in the determination of wage rates. The competitive demand for labour would be most aggressive at school/college leaving age. More management time and effort could be and would have to be channelled into marketing, product design and development as well as long term planning.

The business objective must be profitable continuity which is the driving force of the Japanese.

Whilst Western democracy would not respond to the incentive of avoidance of loss of face, it would react to the fear of failure. A social system that accepts the payment of labour as an unavoidable commitment will do its utmost to use it profitably. In return for the assurance of income, the labourer will accept a discount on his reward to compensate for the elimination of the peaks and troughs of being employed and unemployed. Security has a cost and value. To make economic sense the two must equate, since unless they do social justice remains a pipe dream.

In the forecastable future, the difference between "employment" and "unemployment" will simply be the source of income. The "employed" will be those contributing to the added value of a country. The "unemployed" will not. The greater the national added value, the larger the total source of income. The larger the cake for distribution, the higher the standard of living.

The contributors will be those who have skills and experience required by the country's international economic philosophy. The responsibility of government will be to ensure that all the resources (including labour) are available at the right time, of the right quality and in the right quantity to assist the nation in its progress towards the fulfilment of its ultimate reality.

Let us return finally to the definition of "work". It could be reasonably argued that work as practised and preached in the United Kingdom over the last two hundred years has been as much a battlefield as the idiocy of the Somme. The industrial and political leaders have had as much ability and sensitivity as the Field Marshalls and Generals who ordered their men into bloody battle. Men have died swiftly and in agony or slowly and painfully from industrial accident and disease. Men have been stripped of their self-respect and pride in the pursuit of profit and avoidance of loss. They have been woefully led and deliberately misled.

Those who extol work regardless of its actuality and then despise the brutality of war are forced to draw demarcations of extremes. There is a significant centre ground of struggle for survival and advancement wherein it is impossible to differentiate between morality and necessity.

Imposed and unchosen work is generally a soul destroying exercise. It may be to man's considerable advantage that the Technological Revolution will force him to re-examine and re-define the allocation of his life that he presently calls work. He has been obliged to sell his labour to live within his accepted community. That obligation has become his focal point. After decades of exhortation by employer, politician and union the employee is understandably convinced that wages measure all. They represent what he is worth, what he has and what he is. Yet in addition to the immediate satisfaction of his economic needs, however vital that is, he has grown accustomed to and welcomes the set routine of tasks, effort and recognition. This routine is taken for granted and has become irretrievably interwoven with wages. He cannot have one without the other. The one is the measurement of the other.

If income can be divorced from input (work), entrepreneurs will be able to organise the activity of man as a means of satisfaction in itself. If that were possible then it is just conceivable that work in that form could be as much an ethic as the present use of technically uneconomic time for the purpose of charity and the occupation of surplus (retired) labour.

The difficulty of re-thinking the established concepts of employment, unemployment and work is enormous because the current definitions have been long established by a spectrum of vested interests which, despite their varied objectives, have one common ground. They wish to retain the present status quo, the trenches, the mud and minefields. It will need the irresistible force imposed by unavoidable environmental change to loosen their combined immovable grip. The Technological Revolution is therefore an opportunity that should be quickly and firmly grasped. Technology offers more than comfort and play. It offers freedom from the drudgery of that which has been misrepresented as "work".

Wages, War and Incomes Policies

Wages are measured absolutely, the rate for the job, the cost per hour, the cost per piece and the cost per packet. Wages are recorded absolutely. They become a government statistic that can be manipulated into a mass of meaningless figures. The average weekly wage packet is as much a national standard as a piece of elastic. In isolation, it is a figure of no significance whatsoever, even when compared over a period of time with itself.

Wages are the cost of labour and labour is a productive resource whose reward is determined by its value. Value can only be relative since it is a measurement of one attribute against another.

There is a further dimension. The recipient is as interested in the relative value of his wages as the employer. The latter is concerned with what he gets for his money. The former is interested in what he can buy with his remuneration. For him, wages are more than the means of survival. They should provide a choice of alternative means of satisfaction.

A considerable amount of time is spent in the evaluation of wages as an input cost. The facts in that area are constantly researched and there are many sources of statistics which vary in quality and reliability. There is, however, relatively little effective research into the use to which wages are put. Statistics are blurred by social demarcation, varying preference patterns, the impact of taxation which is far from equitable and the contribution that might be made directly or indirectly by the welfare state. Yet the key value of wages is in the assessment of the satisfaction derived when they are spent. Only then can the recipient gauge the degree of satisfaction against the extent of the effort.

The value of labour as far as the employer is concerned is its contribution towards the creation of added value. That he seldom makes known to the employee usually to avoid encouragement of demands for increased wages. The absence of communication leads to inevitable distrust so that the defence in the late 1970's and early 1980's that there were insufficient profits available to satisfy wage demands were rejected except in cases where insolvency cast its unambiguous shadow.

The absence of any information connecting the added value resulting from the application of labour with the satisfaction derived from the labourer's reward allowed trade unions to obtain support for demands for wage increases based solely on cost of living statistics. That measure was itself erroneous and misleading being concerned only with the moving annual index of prices. But the employers and government were hoist on their own petard. Trade union negotiators were presented with the substance of a very simple argument which even the very least amongst their members could understand. The logic was indisputable. The cost of the shopping basket had gone up over twelve months by a government published amount. The workers were working as hard as ever. The least they deserved was to be able to buy the same basket.

Lost in the political wash were the jewels of relativity. No attempt had been made to equate the value created by labourer with the value of the standard of life that he enjoyed. Standards had been created to protect a number of vested interests, standards that had very little economic sense. A false weapon will often injure more seriously those who seek to defend themselves with it than those they seek to attack.

Wages became interwoven into the rope for a tug of war between political parties. It was a massive game since all between school and retirement age had to accept involvement. Since wages are paid for services rendered, it was quite natural for payer and payee to accept persuasion that a little more effort or money might be equitable. The professional persuader in the form of a politician exhorted the participants and the result was inevitable. The tug of war had become a vicious conflict fostered by greed and envy in which all have suffered and no-one will benefit.

Work in one form or another has existed since man decided to survive. It has been his contribution towards the translation of raw materials into useful products. The activity was sometimes dangerous, usually filthy and often degrading. Work had to be elevated into a religious ethic and identified as the privilege of

99

man. The worker was given a choice. He could opt for loyalty to his boss or loyalty to his community. He could move towards the feudal or the quasi-religious system. He was encouraged to have the good things in life, a wife, a family and a roof. He gathered in the necessities and became inextricably woven into the economic fabric of his society. For centuries, the relationship between the payer and the recipient of wages changed very little, whether in agriculture or in later times in industry and commerce, as observed from Cobbett to Dickens. It is futile to argue whether the Agrarian revolution had more or less effect upon society than the Industrial revolution in much the same way as to attempt to differentiate between the impact on society of fire and the wheel. It appears likely, however, that there will be no doubt as to the significance of the Technological revolution during the second half of the century if, of course, it leaves any society. Work will have to be completely redefined for those whose ancestors had no occasion to even question its need let alone its meaning. In the meantime, democracy continues to be bedevilled by the political distortion of wages and it cannot afford to wait for a re-definition of the concept of work.

Why are wages paid? Because the payer believes that the use of labour so paid has transformed some material into products that he can sell at a price greater than the total cost he has incurred — the same being said of a service. This brings us directly to the concept of added value. We can then answer the question, "How much is paid as wages?" As far as the entrepreneur is concerned the answer is simple. He is obliged to buy in goods and services over which he has little control as to levels of prices. The selling price he sets for that which he produces may also be beyond his control. The difference between what he has to accept as input price and output price is the margin out of which he can pay his workers, the suppliers of his capital and himself. His first obligation in the division of added value is to the provider of his capital in the form of interest and the creation of a fund for its repayment. That which remains is available for the satisfaction of both himself and his workers.

So far so good, but the logic has again ignored the attitude of the recipient, namely, why are the wages acceptable? The answer is again straightforward. The payee believes that he cannot do better elsewhere. If he could he would. But what about all the encouragement towards training, apprenticeship and skills? There was indeed a time when a craft was beneficial, when a skill would be saleable during a lifetime but such opportunities no longer exist. Even when they did, the skills were of little real benefit to their owners.

In the early days of the Industrial revolution certain processes varied little over many decades. A father could pass his job onto his son by the simple method of teaching him the particular skills needed for its execution. In that way he could obtain security for two generations, but even then he could not ensure a good wage. During the eighteenth and nineteenth centuries hosts of skills were developed and taught that never received the rewards to which they were economically entitled. Foundries, potteries, glassworks, engineers — the list has been remarked upon elsewhere. Apprenticeships were a joke, even during the first half of the twentieth century, and often a means of cheap labour. To attempt any apportionment of responsibility for this hypocrisy would be to enter the political lists and that would be beyond the scope of this book. Yet it is a matter of considerable concern that the example of the "old days" as seen through idealistic spectacles by those who by age and experience had no knowledge of such matters is presented as the panacea for labour problems that arise from quite different causes to those experienced in the past. Reducing wages to reflect the economic value of trainees will not solve unemployment any more than apprenticeships in the early twentieth century avoided the unemployment of the 1920's and 1930's.

But time is now against us. In the past there was time to learn a skill and enjoy it, even though it was never adequately rewarded. Industry consistently abused its apprenticeship schemes so that little is lost with their demise. Today's skill is no longer tomorrow's security.

Stripped of its political clothing, the future for work looks bleak. In reality there is much to be done and all of it economic. The problem is not one of availability but an attitude of mind. The nation has been confused by two schools of conditioning. On one side, Great Britain is exposed as a nation of would-be layabouts, work-shy and led by Trade Unions to self-destruction. On the other side, there are those who insist that Great Britain is dominated by the exploiters of the poor and oppressed, who misapply the honest endeavours of their fellow creatures who in turn had the misfortune to be born without privilege. The words are evocative, emotional and completely prejudiced. If either description were accurate, then Great Britain had no past and certainly has no future. If actuality is a combination of both then the country may have had a past of sorts, a facade over a deep hypocrisy, but still has no future of any attraction for its inhabitants.

The economic truth is fortunately neither one description or the other or any combination of both. The answer for the future, as it has always been, is War. Not with bows and arrows, machine guns or atomic bombs, but in the sense understood and practised by Japan. Economically war has always been beneficial, even to the loser. Nations have benefited in terms of their societies, standards of living and regeneration. In the past, the costs of these benefits have been morally unacceptable and religiously offensive — even though God has often been assumed to be the guiding spirit of opposing soldiers.

Economically, however, there is no argument. The unification of a nation through fear has led to innumerable achievements in development and production that otherwise may never have taken place or at best would have taken centuries in the absence of such motivation. War has destroyed and therefore imposed investment. The survival of the strong has strengthened people.

If, therefore, the moral and social objections are removed, the imposition of external necessity brought about by conflict to avoid defeat and oppression might well create a unification of effort and determination. Whether the Western world likes it or not, the challenge is already there and unless accepted overtly, the result will be as degrading as the loss of a formal conflict.

It may well be that peace in the accepted sense cannot be propogated by the politicians of developed countries for the simple reason that the production of weapons of war constitutes a vital part of their economies. In what else could they invest? How otherwise could they generate fear and from fear the gift of power? But once again the object of this book is not to examine political and social policies as to their motivation or intent. Suffice it to say that it may not be in the interests of political leaders to establish a long-lasting environment of peaceful co-existence.

Fortunately for the populace, economic war is in fact political war and acceptable as a means of garnering power, so the remainder of this argument will find political support.

It is the relationship between Wages and War which may prove too sensitive for public accord.

War is the concentration of economic resources with a set schedule of priorities to achieve one specific end. It requires supreme concentration and the elimination of any irrelevant, unnecessary or non-contributory activities and/or resources. Demand is totally elastic as the products that are created are destroyed. Supply is controlled and directed.

Virtually it transforms a democracy into a dictatorship by universal agreement.

In these conditions, wages are consistently related to the value of their contribution. Since labour is also directed, its application is optimised. The supply of labour is diminished, a substantial proportion being enlisted. The scenario is totally unaccepted and unacceptable as a means of political fulfilment. But there is very little difference between war as waged since the time of the Roman empire and that which is facing Western democracy over the next few hundred years. The existence of the nuclear weapon has eliminated the gauntlet across the face. Provocation is today a sibilant secret and its anticipatory ignorance is as terrifying as Pearl Harbour.

The advantage of economic war as an alternative to total war is that the former is a means of achieving economic power which can ultimately lead to total power, but it need not go that far. It does not conflict with religious beliefs and the impression of independence. It is far more likely to enjoy a lengthy period of success and victory is not achieved one day and responsibility for the defeated unavoidably assumed the next. Victory can be won by stealth and enjoyed at leisure.

The first requirement in any war is justification. That for the Western world is easy. Its economy is already under threat and in many ways it has already been invaded. There are no moral problems in responding to that threat.

The second requirement is leadership to concentrate the minds and efforts of those who are essential in achieving a successful outcome. The first task is to make all aware of the danger and with the support of their fear to set out a plan of campaign. Power has to be given to those who lead to enable them to commandeer the resources that are needed for the task. Fear of aggression is a far more potent motivator than pride and greed which are necesssary for the aggressor in the persuasion of his followers.

The final requirement is success. Unlike total war, economic war can be a never ending struggle where success is gained first by one side and then the other. The defeats eliminate any complacency and strengthen the argument of those who wish to lead. Again, unlike total war, the fall-out of economic war can be extremely beneficial to those not directly involved in the struggle. Countries which have raw materials needed by the combatants enjoy a competitive demand and more attractive prices. Even the most lowly nations discover that their geographic location and labour force can provide certain attractions from which they can benefit.

Those who find the suggestion that the prime task of mankind is to engage in economic war unacceptable for whatever reason other than economic, should consider the arguments put forward supporting conflicts which are acceptable. Introvert dissention which degenerates into class conflict, religious disagreements, oppression of humanity and destruction of the environment are physically and morally defended to the death. No-one need die as a result of economic warfare.

Economics is the basic activity of man who when he has made himself comfortable can afford principles. In the course of creating that comfort, there will be many advisors as to the ways in which he might enjoy the fruits of his endeavours. All will seek to participate. Man is a natural combatant. Whilst he may not enjoy the fight, he certainly savours the success that might be achieved.

Work was elevated and placed upon a pedestal as an ethic to encourage those whose efforts were needed to accept terms and conditions which were unrelated to the value of their potential contribution. And why not, since there is no morality in economics? There is no point in paying more than is necessary for any resource and if persuasion or presentation can reduce a cost, then so be it.

It would therefore seem quite logical that that which has been worshipped for three hundred years should now be replaced by a more up-to-date idol. Economic warfare would appear to be an emminent successor to work.

Incomes Policy

The spectre of incomes policy haunts every political leader in the UK. They pay lip service to segments of a spectrum that ranges from no policy at all to one of absolute governmental imposition. When pressed to explain the practicalities of their respective policies, all are reduced to hesitant and often inane qualification that translates vague theory into irrelevant possibilities. The stumbling block is the blind adherence to a correlation between income and inflation, based upon the erroneous assumption that the performance of the worker remains constant regardless of changes in his wage packet.

An effective incomes policy measures and monitors four values which are:

(a) The currency denomination of wages.

(b) The satisfaction value of wages.

(c) The added value attributable to wages.

(d) The relationship between added value, its proportion of labour value and the effect of prices on added value.

Concentration upon average wages paid achieves nothing. Its practical interpretation is a farce. The determination of an "acceptable" percentage increase is ludicrous. Its relationship with price movement is but one dimension and as such can be quite misleading.

Past so-called income policies are as relevant to future domestic strategy as single-entry book-keeping is to double- entry accounting. There must be an awareness in statistical terms of the fact that wages represent a standard of living and also contribute to the creation of wealth. It would appear both equitable and natural for the two dimensions to increase at the same rate so that the equation balances.

The behaviour pattern is clearly discernible. The payee will judge the reasonableness of his reward in terms of what it will buy against the cost of his effort. The payer will assess the fairness of the payment by measuring the relationship between labour input costs and the wealth it creates in terms of added value. Since added value is directly affected by prices which also directly affect the purchasing power of wages, the system can be balanced.

An incomes policy is an essential economic tool not to set wages by any predetermined criteria but to enable those in power to monitor and measure a vital part of domestic economic policy, namely the effective use of the resource of labour. The need for a specific and isolated system is that the consequences of ineffective, inequitable or uneconomic use of labour are far more costly than similar inefficiency in the use of any other resource. An imbalance between recipient and user satisfaction can lead to many complications and economic disruptions. Labour has power to vote. It can destroy itself and others. It is volatile. It is unique. For that reason alone it demands a solus system of measurement — hence an incomes policy.

Post 1985 a possible statement of government intent would be to ensure as far as is practicable that the satisfaction value of income will rise commensurate with the increase in added value. At least the country would be putting into effect by choice and pre-determination that which has occurred in the past through error, omission and conflict.

There is one vital element of an incomes policy that warrants an absolute figure. That is the statutory minimum wage which provides a base for:

(a) Calculation of the standard "unemployment" wage.

(b) Encouragement of the employer to apply labour economically.

(c) Elimination of marginally economic labour applications such as low priced goods sweat shops.

Whilst the statutory minimum wage is an absolute figure, it has considerable relative effect for the benefit of the total economic system. It can be argued that, by historic com-parison, the higher the statutory minimum wage and the greater the gap between it and the standard "unemployment" wage, the greater the advantage that can be gained in that it ensures and rewards maximum effort. Employers who are obliged to pay high wages will expect equivalent results. They will be encouraged to apply labour sparingly and effectively. There is also little doubt but that generally those who work prefer to exert effort in return for a commensurate reward.

The alternative of a low-wage economy is economic nonsense and political suicide. It breeds disincentive, dissent and discord. It reduces the indigenous standard of living, discourages investment, encourages short-term opportunism and exploitation. Even the most astute businessman regards it as a temporary initial step towards a more efficient use of his resources. It is a political expedient that is transparently false and unworthy of any serious economic consideration.

The Role of The Trade Unions

The role of the trade unions in an industrial society was clearly defined and confirmed during the Industrial Revolution. Union banners proclaimed the defence of the worker against exploitation. Of all the resources of production, human beings were unique and needed protection, entirely of course for their own good. Christian principles were evoked to unify the lower classes and resist the blandishments of the new race of employers. Leaders of the unions were undoubtedly genuine in their motives and charged by the righteousness of their cause. They had ample evidence to confirm the fears that they expressed on behalf of others. The greed and avarice of those who wished to manipulate the wealth of the nation provided a broad enough stream of examples of exploitation. The ethic of work was thrust forward as the prime objective and the Christian satisfaction of man. Preachers travelled far and wide to spread the gospel of manufacture and lead willing hands from field to furnace. Hypocrisy was a vital trait of Victorian society and the cornerstone of the Free Church democracy.

It may be argued that but for the trade unions, the United Kingdom's labour force would have degenerated into slave labour. Economically, let alone socially through the intervention of religion in one form or another, that could not have happened simply because the consequences would have been contrary to the long term interests of the creators of wealth. There is no doubt that given no hindrance or objection the pattern would have been subjugation, bending of knees and touching forelocks to establish everyone's place in the order of things. But even with that achieved people in the mass would not have been encouraged to give of their best. Dictatorship whether left, right or centre, is ultimately uneconomic as is indeed democracy as defined in the 1980's. A far more likely outcome in the absence of organised labour would have been a feudal system based on the lines of the Quakers or the Japanese. Who is to say that these systems have been uneconomic and socially unsuccessful?

The U.K. economy has had one saving grace. It has never been completely dependent on any one resource, other than its people. This has had two consequences. The first was the unhealthy interest of power seekers in the control of people. The second was an estoppel on the destruction of the economy. The list of past and present national resources is most impressive, there being virtually no gap between the identification and exploitation of each. It started with timber, arable land and fish, then expanded with coal, iron and steel, culminating with oil and gas. The British were quite unable despite their very best endeavours to destory their economy in the way in which they had wasted those of dependent nations who had had the misfortune to have the custody of but one major resource, in addition of course to their people.

As it was, the United Kingdom had an abundance of all that it needed in terms of natural and human resources to support itself. The mixture which provided its economic strength made for a complex and complicated society which could not respond easily to any change requiring re-allocation of resources. Industry established itself with very deep roots, representing security and a routine way of living. Labour, having once been removed from the country of the town, dug in.

No matter how appalling the conditions, familiarity breeds preference. Despite the protestations of politicians and the efforts of planners, labour froze into immobility. The rigidity spread up the ladder and management became limited in breadth and experience. Confidence was not based upon competence but derived from the success of past generations. Expertise was protected and isolated from technology. The military hierarchy structure adopted by industrial organisations was accentuated by an educational system that segregated and then committed individuals into courses over which they had little or no control to influence. The social structure imposed the ultimate grid within which all became constrained. The United Kingdom had successfully imprisoned itself and trade unions were by no means the least amongst the offenders.

109

The power of any trade union is determined by the extent of the need for the resource that it represents. That need is governed by the entrepreneurial profit created from the use of the resource as an essential ingredient in a mixture of resources. In the short term the profit may be such that labour can command an inordinate price so that the power of the union is enormous. Yet there lies in the significance of that profit an inherent danger to the long term power of the union. First, whilst it continues the entrepreneur will seek as a matter of urgency alternative means of production, although in the short term he continues to give way to inordinate demands. The trade union becomes bloated with power and blind through self deception. Secondly the entrepreneur knows that whilst exceptional profits are achieved by being first in the market place, competition must surely arise and that sooner or later the continuity of acceptable profits will depend on his control and eventual minimisation of costs. The mix and relative efficiency of the use of resources will come under close scrutiny and that could occur just when the union, brim full of confidence, is putting forward its maximum demands made on past capitulations. The bluff is called and the power lost.

The contribution of Trade Unions is by no means easy to define. Their objectives would at first sight appear to be quite straight-forward and primarily centred about the protection of their members. It will be argued that the lot of their members is infinitely better than that which it was, say a hundred years ago. That is certainly so in some instances, but even there can the unions claim the real credit? Little boys and girls no longer work in mines or clamber up chimneys, but is that the result of trade union interference or intervention by politicians seeking votes on the nineteenth century bandwagon of religious revival? It could even be argued that the unions had a vested interest in eliminating child labour if only to avoid cheap sources of labour developing from the ranks of those who since childhood had accepted low wages and rotten conditions as a normal way of life. Perhaps the attitude of trade unions towards animals could have been influenced by their views on mechanisation. That still leaves the great majority of practices which have survived and flourished despite the protestations and exhortations of union leaders.

Conditions of employment in a large number of primary and secondary industries remained appalling right up to their demise.

Despite political propoganda, wages paid in the United Kingdom were, and still are, quite inadequate. If there is any doubt as to these accusations, then application to anyone who has actually worked in any of the following industries in Great Britain will confirm their validity:- heavy engineering, gas works, glass works, foundries, mines (of all sorts, shapes and sizes), wood-working, tanning, weaving, metal fabrication, building — the list is long. It will be said that the nature of these industries is such that improvements in working conditions are either uneconomic or impracticable and that may well be so. However, that will only support the main argument that for whatever reasons, the Trade Unions have had only a marginal effect in the protection of their members through a wide band of industrial society. The irony is that their real contribution to the well-being of their members was outside the day to day activities in shops and factories. Their first effective effort was to organise and develop the Co-Operative Society system. This provided their members with the economic benefits derived from a unique strength. The customer may be king, but where he commands and delivers service he can truly enjoy power.

Their second effective action was to provide and encourage worker education. This generated the articulate and persuasive leader. It also created the Labour Party which then capitalised on its skills by creating for its leaders a new and more profitable role in politics as opposed to industry. The rise of the socialist politician ensured the demise of worker education for the benefit of the unions. That which had been understood by the ruling classes for centuries had at last been made clear to those who sought to usurp them. Education is the cornerstone of power and without it the edifice cannot be sustained.

As far as their efforts in industry and commerce were concerned, the unions were effective only as far as the market place allowed. Where comnpetition was fierce, unions pontificated but remained powerless. Sweat shops survived and flourished where economic pressures outweighed political ideals. As for their major platform, wage increases were spasmodic, unplanned, opportunistic and to a large extent linked with blackmail. More often than not, wage demands were irresponsible with the inevitable long term effect of labour substitution. Despite the superficial inordinate increases in wages "negotiated" during the 1960's and 1970's, the United

Kingdom remained a lowly member of the income league of Western developed countries. In real terms, the standard of living of the working classes never reflected the inherent wealth and potential of Great Britain. The combination of misdirected socialist policies and the ambitions of union leaders ensured that countless opportunities presented to the nation post 1945 were either ignored altogether or frittered away carelessly and without any forethought.

To summarise thus far, it is suggested that in their overt intentions Trade Unions achieved very little for themselves and their members over and above that which would have been offered in any event. Their main contribution was to accelerate that which would have been determined by the economic environment. On the other hand, their achievements albeit for a relatively short period in their apparently secondary activities, such as education and the Co-Ops, were significant.

There is another aspect of the past role of trade unions in the United Kingdom. In their concentration on the improvement of the wage packet of their members, they contributed to a disastrous history of self-deception and destruction. Many years ago, the industrialist had accepted that the value of labour related only to its output and had concentrated on the piece-work system as a means of payment by results. If the worker produced, he was paid. Labour costs were classified as direct and indirect or productive and non-productive. From 1930 onwards, bargaining in times per job instead of wage per week dominated pay determination and heralded the arrival of the time and motion expert. Pence per piece became the universal norm. Initially, Trade Unions resisted work measurement, not because they believed it would not prove beneficial but they wished to act as the representative for the worker and add to their power. The quid pro quo for their "reluctant" acquiescence was that they should be directly involved in all wage negotiations at grass roots levels. With the added benefit of hindsight, the unions made a very bad strategic mistake. Immersion in wage negotiations left them with only one weapon, the Strike. But at the time involvement added to their overt power and increased their member's packets. Output rose, wages increased and unit costs fell. All seemed more than justified. Then, as production increased, often quite dramatically, management weaknesses in control became apparent and working capital proved inadequate. The direct involvement of Union negotiations with management to the exclusion of the worker, gave rise to mistrust and suspicion. In some industries considerable doubt existed whether middle management was independent or just a facade of union representation. Pressure grew on sales organisations to win larger orders to absorb the increased flow of goods. Prices had to be reduced and problems entirely new to management solved. The leadership of industry had long been the engineer and production manager. By the 1960's they had to give way to the marketing man. He in turn abdicated to the accountant in the 1970's, and as each took the wheel, the problems increased.

Confusion and confrontation reigned. Planning was virtually non-existent and industry staggered from one crisis to another. Piece work degenerated into specialisation, then demarcation and finally job-protection at any price. That which had been introduced to increase efficiency and improve the lot of labour led to its stagnation as an economic resource which in turn delayed the vital appreciation of the need for change and deferred for far too long the introduction of new machines, methods, and ultimately automation.

The myopic approach adopted by unions, management and labour were matched only by the supreme blindness of politicians. Where planning had existed, it had not extended beyond the natural cycle of any given mix of resources. Examples of this logic which produced cycles of exceptional length were to be found originally in the timber and automotive industries, but these were truly exceptions to the general rule. In theory, industry in the United Kingdom planned. In practice, it made no such attempt until the introduction of annual budgets in the 1930's, and the temporary interest in Corporate Planning in the 1960's and 1970's. By the early 1980's, large sections of British industry were concerned solely with survival and that left little time or inclination for crystal-ball gazing. As for politicians, they, as usual, made their invaluable contribution of consistent uncertainty providing six monthly signposts which swivelled according to the prevailing political wind. Their posture was that, whatever their pre-determined course, unforeseeable deviation was unavoidable so that responsibility could not lie with them. Arrival at the desired destination was more a matter of hope than genuine anticipation.

113

The final contribution of the Trade Unions was to ensure that industry and commerce should provide a political battlefield. At first, the unions tried in vain to straddle the perimeter. In the end they had to decide whether to join in the battle or to become a spectator. On the advice of their politically ambitious brethren they decided wrongly on the former. It was a natural error but it ensured that their economic power would diminish and with that their influence on political policies. As long as Trade Unions see their role in society as one confined to class warfare on the industrial battlefield, their real contribution to those they purport to protect will become more and more limited and finally one of self strangulation.

In order that Trade Unions can make an economic contribution to society, it is suggested that they should take heed of the lessons of the past, examine them with integrity and relate their findings to an equally honest interpretation of the future.

Perhaps the most obvious comment is that unions represent a potent political force so that an additional party to represent the worker is both superfluous and self-destructive. The role of the unions in industry post 1986 may well not include wage bargaining or the improvement of working conditions. The key factor in economic resources will lie outside the organised labour market. Profits or surplus will accrue for reasons far beyond the control of the worker, or even management, although the dangerous attraction of profit distribution will remain. The baking of the cake is hard work and responsibility; the intriguing exercise of its division is much more exciting. Much time can be allocated to the delightful decision of how much for how many. As far as the economy is concerned it is wasted time and effort.

Unions would do well to abandon their participation even in the baking process. The quality and quantity of ingredients, the quality of the cooking utensils and the reliability of essential services are in truth only marginally within their control. Unions might even be the cause of an inferior product, or at least delay its final presentation. Too many cooks, possibly. And in that comment there lies an overwhelming reason why it might be to the benefit of society as a whole if Trade Unions transformed their approach to one of political endeavour rather than industrial intervention. The analogy of the United Kingdom as a bustling kitchen presents an apparently complete picture, with a cook merrily mixing ingredients and

114

turning out a succession of aromatic cakes. But there is a figure missing. Who appointed the cook? Who acquired for the cook's use the ingredients, utensils and oven? It can only be that ubiquitous and much maligned character, the entrepreneur and he has in reality the greatest in the size of the cake, and that is what really matters. Is it practicable for Trade Unions to get out of the kitchen and match the function of the entrepreneur?

Before pursuing that question further, some consideration should be given as to why Trade Unions should in the first instance abandon their role in the environment which gave them birth and in which they feel most comfortable. The analogy is apposite. Unions have to grow up or shut up. Their environment has changed almost beyond recognition. There is considerable doubt anyway as to whether their past contribution has had long term benefit which must in turn give rise to further doubt as to the benefits from its continuity. But the over-riding fact is that the kitchen is no longer the centre of the family whose lives will in future be governed more by events outside the house let alone by any particular room. The future of the United Kingdom will be more affected by events and developments without its boundaries. Unions can never effectively represent an economic force whilst they remain enmeshed in the application and use of internal resources. The more the work force and unions are intermingled, the greater their isolation together from the seat of power. The leader must stand apart from the led and the pursuance of equality should not be allowed to destroy the basic tenets of successful organisation. The Trade Unions should be seen to be what they are, a political force representing those who hold similar political views and using their economic muscle to achieve the translation of theory into fact.

A similar example can be found in the Confederation of British Industry. At its inception it was designed to represent all aspects of industry and commerce, both management and labour. Whilst it clung to those ideals, it remained ineffective and mistrusted. Workers simply did not believe that the C.B.I. was anything other than an employer's tool. The greater the protestation, the greater the disbelief. Employers were also put off by the idealistic, and to them impracticable policy. It was only when the C.B.I. overtly and deliberately proposed itself as solidly on the side of management that everyone relaxed and believed. The ethics were unimportant.

If battlelines are clearly drawn then no-one questions who is friend or foe. Everything is as it should be. So the C.B.I. become a force of some power. It exerts some political influence. It stands apart from industry and it can pontificate without being misunderstood.

If the Trade Unions could emulate the C.B.I. and extricate themselves from the ineffective ambiguity of shop floor involvement and become a recognised political body, then they might adopt many roles, all acceptable, inter-related and effective. In that form, their roles could be:-

1. Protecting the political interests of their members in their capacities as people at work.

2. Use their financial muscle to gain political objectives.

3. Initiate direct involvement in the long-term planning of the United Kingdom economy.

4. Observe and evaluate the economic progress of industry and commerce from a point of vantage.

5. Evaluate the future developments in international industry and commerce, their implications and means of achievement.

6. Organise the real assets and wealth of the working people to their advantage.

7. Assist directly in the inevitable changes in society.

To translate generalities into specifics in 1987, political Trade Unions could:-

1. Take the lead in Youth training, education and development.

2. Take the lead in the organisation of transitional training, sabbaticals, post graduate training, and leisure organisation.

3. Organise wholesale, retailing and provisions of services, including health, care and retirement.

4. Take the lead in community matters.

5. Join forces in retirement programmes.

There is no place for the Union of the past in the economy of the future. Dramatic change in the latter requires an equally revolutionary change in the former. That can only be achieved by abstraction and regrouping. Then perhaps industry and society may both benefit.

Post 1987, the British Trade Union movement is offered the opportunity of becoming an economic and political force that could well challenge for government office, provided it is prepared to change, to resist reference to the past and to concentrate on the future.

The movement is capable of representing a complete political spectrum and it is able to organise financial resources. The fact that all its members are actively engaged in the production of wealth in whatever form gives it a unique and immensely strong platform. All its members regardless of colour, education or creed are vitally interested in the economic welfare of the country. Their common objective is that the nation must prosper and that all those who contribute to that prosperity, should enjoy a reasonable return for their endeavours. The way they can achieve that ambition in the modern world is not by offering themselves individually or collectively for work or trying as quasi-industry segments to force short term monetary benefits, but by ensuring as far as they are collectively able that all resources are used as efficiently as possible. The Trade Union movement and its members have the economic power to achieve that, but without education they do not have the capability.

It is not surprising that a number of the present Trade Union leaders would resolutely oppose, either overtly or covertly, improvements in the education and understanding of their followers since ignorance in others is the best assurance of continuation of their personal power. Nevertheless, unless unions accept the challenge of self-improvement and their leaders rely upon integrity and competence in retaining their positions, the opportunity will be obscured by the red mists of rhetoric and oratorical clangour. The routing of the opposition parties in the 1987 General Election clearly demonstrates the urgent need for an alternative credible government and that could well be filled by a Trade Union movement that is a true political body representing an economic interest, people.

Nationalisation Versus Privatisation

Before the emergence of a Socialist Party, public ownership of utilities appeared to be divorced from politics. The reasons put forward for such ownership were generally accepted as being to ensure the continuity of essential services for the community as a whole and to avoid the abuse of monopoly powers.

These social objectives overcame any free market opposition and the weak, albeit the majority, were protected against the strong. Economic justification was added in the argument that the effective use of a community's resources ultimately benefited that community and all those who worked within it, so even those who gave up their individual rights joined in the subsequent gains.

To the more cynical observer however the actual transfer of assets from private enterprise into public ownership occurred after the harvest had been garnered and only the problem of straw disposal remained.

Unbridled competition had long since eroded marginal profits. The entrepreneur had overstretched himself and by the transfer had been saved from the otherwise inevitable consequences of his greed and lack of investment.

The attractions of public ownership or nationalisation as it became labelled later were overwhelming for those who sought to represent the ordinary working man. In the first instance, industries that obviously qualified for such attention were labour intensive, outmoded and inefficient. They represented votes and an opportunity for the fulfilment of pre-election promises. A government elected manifesto. Furthermore, if it were a socialist government it could and would ensure agreeable conditions of employment as well as the capital that was needed to resuscitate that which was almost dead. The question of a painless release and quiet interment never arose. Politically, out of date industry was manna from heaven, and nationalisation was "in". This policy was accepted by both the established U.K. political parties, since those who supported the Conservatives were of the same mind as their forebears in the nineteenth century. The future for a number of long established industries was very bleak and unattractive. Industrialists who were sufficiently long-sighted could see the possibility that after a spell of reconstruction and massive investment, some if not all of those industries might be transformed into attractive investment situations ready for another cycle of exploitation.

Nationalisation suffered some token resistance from the Conservative simply because they could not be seen to agree with their opponents in public. Their motives might have been questioned. Economists could see no practical alternatives. Consequently it became the standard of the Labour Party under which it swept to power in 1945 and remained a rallying point until the arrival of the Thatcher government in 1979.

Three decades of nationalisation had been long enough for the dust to settle and the identities of possible phoenixes to emerge. The time was ripe for the return of freed, revitalised and refreshed industrial concerns to their former owners. The pendulum had swung sufficiently so that there was political mileage in the proposition that certain industries should be privatised — the new "in" word. Industry was no longer labour intensive. Votes would instead be harvested from the great mass of the populace that could be conditioned by advertising campaigns aimed at the desire for something for nothing. The smaller the investor, the larger his number. So a formula was devised by which as many individuals as possible could be induced to purchase tiny parcels of shares which would show a substantial profit on paper thereby encouraging the holders to retain their investment indefinitely. Future company meetings would provide invaluable propaganda platforms for preaching the continuity of private ownership ensured by the cross in the appropriate slot on the political voting slip. If the well established lethargy of a company shareholder could be harnessed and applied as an estoppel on votes cast for the political left, then the future of the right would be assured.

Had the Thatcher government left matters there then it is likely that the strategy would have succeeded. Renationalisation would have been virtually impossible for a number of reasons and politically it would have been suicidal. But fortunately for the electorate, the politician had gone a little too far along the road of self protection and glorification. In short, he had been too clever for his own good.

Privatisation accomplished a unique element known as the golden share. At first sight it was a brilliant compromise whereby the government could realise virtually the whole of its investment at a thumping profit and still retain ultimate control through peculiar voting powers attached to the golden share. Its creation enabled the Conservative government to silence at one stroke of the pen all its critics who were declaiming the loss of control of vital industries. The government no longer had to retain at least 51% of the action and the monetary rewards arising from this innovation were extremely substantial. Someone, somewhere had had a brilliant idea and presumably was suitably rewarded. The Treasury could enjoy the satisfaction of cake with cream and still hold the pastry for future digestion.

The political and economic implications of privatisation have been obscured by the assumption that it is but a phase in the never ending tug-of-war between those who believed the rope would stand the strain for ever. In truth, the rope has broken and the contest will have to be resumed with different gear.

In the first instance it is debatable in economic terms whether privatisation in its original form differed basically from nationalisation. When public ownership was promoted, paper money was issued in exchange for paper certificates. The underlying transaction was the exchange of a current liability for a long term asset. The Treasury endeavoured to reduce the cost of the consideration by collecting taxes on the use of the money issued, the income being used to resuscitate the assets required until they could hopefully earn profits which would again be absorbed by the Treasury.

On privatisation, the Treasury collected paper money in exchange for paper certificates and endeavoured to use that money to reduce government borrowing thereby effectively generating capital. The underlying transaction was that the public had handed over one asset in return for another.

The only significant difference between the two transactions was that which had happened between the two events. During that time, the assets had been extensively modified and improved as a profit making entity. The taxpayer had indirectly provided venture capital. The investor on privatisation, who was also the taxpayer, added a further contribution in the form of a capital profit which was pocketed by the Treasury. *Plus ça change . . .* The political labels of nationalisation and privatisation covered the same transaction, the reallocation of a country's wealth for the benefit of those identified by government, the prime beneficiary being those in power at the time. The musical chairs could in theory have continued indefinitely, until the aberration of the golden share which opened up a completely new ball game.

The creation of the golden share was intended to provide the protagonists of privatisation with an incontrovertible defence against the accusation that a sale of more than 49% of an organisation's equity would damage national security and could lead to the loss of an invaluable national asset. Since the Conservative government had used the excuse of national interests to thwart certain embarrassing attacks and had enthusiastically defended national assets when predators appeared, the accusation was difficult to duck. The golden share was undoubtedly a brilliant move.

Its characteristics were ideal for the role envisaged by its supporters. The golden share was an entrepreneurial weapon. It provided very considerable power in return for very little investment. It encompassed a vast vote that outweighed all the votes of the army of small investors who were its co-shareholders. It had nothing to lose if the company failed other than the value of its power and that was of little consequence when the company had become worthless. But above all it represented power limited only by the discretion of those who designed it and gave it birth. No one else had any say in its constitution. It was there and unless it was accepted by all and sundry, nothing else would happen. All the profits directly or indirectly attributable to the act of privatisation could not emerge unless the golden share was accepted, warts and all. Like Cromwell, a slight impediment can be easily overlooked if the beauty of the visage is secondary to the usefulness of its owner. In particular when the power so attained would only be used in the public interests. Since profits were now and only vague dangers might be in the future, it was no contest. The golden share was eagerly grasped by the politicians.

But the principle remains for all to see. That which has long been practised in the so called private sector is now used in the public sector to attain a political advantage. Special shares with special powers are sometimes thrust forward as one of the unacceptable features of capitalism. The London Stock Exchange has long been critical of extraordinary shares except of course for those companies that are long established and highly profitable. Power can be and often is misapplied. That is those who have not gained by its application often accuse those who have benefited by its abuse. But the responsibility of the golden share is far greater than that attached to its present use. The Thatcher government has devised a new political tool in the execution of its economic aims. It is designed to do a particular job but its characteristics are such that it can be provided with a number of cutting devices that would transform it into quite a different implement. The irony may well be that the political party that prides itself on non intervention in the free economy, that advocates the survival of the strong and reward for hard work and endeavour, has introduced into the political arena a weapon that the free economy has wielded happily and profitably for itself and had no intention of broadcasting its potential to those who might have entirely different ideas and ambitions.

To illustrate the implications of this mechanism let us consider the reaction of an entrepreneur to this device and the ways in which he might be disposed to use it for his own benefit. The brief is simple. The entrepreneur can create a share that does not exist in any company in which he may or may not have an interest and that share can contain any conditions he may care to insert. Where he has an interest, it is probable that 51% of the votes will suffice since he can decide quite unilaterally when he can use those votes and the reason can be as vague as in his personal (national) interest. That should be wide enough. But suppose that he is intent upon the acquisition of a company in which he presently has no interest. His brief is such that instead of buying all the equity of that company, he need only insert the golden share into the equity structure of that company. The other shareholders can complain on the grounds that he has not bothered even to offer for their shares but since he had that power he only chose not to use it so their complaints are as ineffective as the voices of 49%.

An interesting development of this new concept is that having been forged from the experience of those directly engaged in the free market, it is almost certain that the politicians who have adopted it and who have become aware of its two edged nature will seek advice again from the same resource as to the means by which it might be contained and restrained.

That advice will be complex and complicated. One of the most difficult exercises in commercial law is the creation of precedent and statute to maintain a well established and fundamental principle yet at the same time protect against its misapplication and abuse. The cases for the latter are legion and signify that it is almost impossible to achieve. In those exceptional circumstances when protection has been granted, the costs incurred have been excessive.

It may be that the Thatcher government through its own entrepreneurial ability has created a means whereby any government of any colour can take over, control or realise any corporate entity within its jurisdiction without the costs or problems previously encountered. The cycle of acquisition, resuscitation and realisation is here to stay and the mechanics have been streamlined both as to effectiveness and cost. It took an entrepreneur to achieve that end and a politician to grasp the implications and ensure its implementation. The significant common ground for the two is that both are concerned with the short term and the latter will undoubtedly live to rue that fact.

As is too often the case, political expediency imposed to achieve economic ends encourages in the medium and long term exactly the opposite of that which was intended. The golden share emerged as a means of facilitating privatisation, the very antithesis of public ownership. It is the ultimate entrepreneurial weapon of an entrepreneurial government. But the entrepreneur is not confined to any particular political party. It is true that those who believe in public ownership, for whatever reason and ambition, have not demonstrated the equivalent imagination and originality of their political opponents. Nevertheless it cannot be conceived that they will overlook the opportunity and pass it by. Government itself has given itself a very sharp set of economic teeth. It is not beyond the bounds of probability that one day the biter may get bit.

The Machiavellian view is therefore quite clear. Privatisation and nationalisation are the political tags applied to the same economic exercise — the redistribution of wealth.

The expectation is that the redistribution will result in an increase in the overall wealth of the nation which in practice is extremely unlikely because the main purpose is political. The left make no attempt to disguise their objective, citing social advantages as their *raison d'etre*. The right wing politician puts forward the benefits derived from private enterprise as justification for the claim of an increase in national wealth. Yet when all political facades are stripped away, the net economic outcome is the translation of a long term debt into a current asset. Balance sheet movements do not of themselves change the net equity value of a company any more than they improve the wealth of a national economy.

Industries will emerge, grow and decay regardless of political ambitions. Their ownership is important only in so far as it determines the utilisation of assets which have outlived their usefulness. It is unlikely that, beyond the short term, politicians, whatever their hue, will adopt different policies since the outcome is inevitable and can only be delayed.

During the second half of the 1980's, the Thatcher government will add to its privatisation scalps. Two obvious victims will be Electricity and Water, both highly essential commodities and both of economic and social significance. They are indeed key monopolies.

By 1990, the British economy will have been transformed and bear little comparison with the economy even of the 1960's. It will merit direct comparison with the United States economy if not in size, then in constitution. The stage after privatisation must be fragmentation. Each private monopolistic empire will be segmented as "management buy-outs" and the capitalist process repeated. In this way, the government will hope to exercise some influence by regionalisation and/or specialisation. The argument will be the need for competition. The reason will be that the politician will begin to regret the loss of industrial power. This process may well take another decade and will assist in ensuring the continuance of a Conservative government unless there is a radical rethink amongst the opposing political parties.

Armaments and Economics

Men are the fodder of war. Armaments are the fodder of politicians. There cannot be a more attractive situation for a budding politician than the continued fear of total war and its non-realisation.

The threat of aggression justifies the investment of a large proportion of a nation's wealth on terms and conditions designed entirely by those in power. As long as war remains a threat the politician has a double chance of maintaining continuity of office. In the first instance he can encourage the populace to look towards him as their protector. The more powerful aspect of his position, however, is that he has under his discretion and control an almost unlimited proportion of a country's wealth to direct and manipulate as he pleases.

The irony of the Western world's phobia post 1945 is that the losers of the Second World War have been forced to remove all pretence at the necessity for defence and consequently in their national productive development. In the case of Japan, the philosophy applied and the methods of application of the country's total wealth have been similar to those which have been adopted by their wartime conquerors in the use of their marginal wealth set aside overtly for armaments.

With the exception of Japan, and to some extent Western Germany, all the developed economies have taken the sublimely easy route of insisting that peace from 1945 to 1985 is directly attributable to a continued investment in and the development of nuclear weapons, the ultimate deterrent. Politicians are notorious for the acquisition of responsibility for success, and also for the identification of unrelated cause and effect to support their protestations. The community as a whole should not, therefore, be surprised at the paucity of their logic. It is true that for a short period of time, probably no more than a decade and terminating with man's first venture on the moon, the mutuality of destruction was an extremely effective deterent. The essential decisions, however, were politically pragmatic both during and after the period when the threat of nuclear war was real.

The rub of the matter is that in the long term the economic consequences of a continuance of this charade are almost as expensive as those from which mankind is supposedly protected. It is likely that the present Russian leadership will appreciate that quickly and seek in the 1990's to break the circle. It will then be too late to prevent Japanese economic domination of the West, but it could still pre-empt Chinese economic domination of the East.

But, if the consequences are so damaging, why do the politicians perpetuate the myth? Two of the reasons have been stated earlier, namely the generation of fear to attract the support of votes and secondly the power to direct a considerable proportion of a country's wealth wheresoever they please. In addition to these, however, they would feel obliged to find an economic answer to the replacement of warfare, and that would be exceedingly difficult. Armaments are consumable at will by destruction or obsolescence. Armaments create employment. Armaments encourage research and development. Armaments support law and order within as well as without a country.

The construction of a modern weapon such as a military aeroplane provides employment for very many people of varying skills and capabilities. At first sight the raw material content would appear to be relatively slight in physical terms. In fact production of the extremely high grade components is itself a long and expensive process. But the ancillary employment is remarkable. Computers, drawing office equipment, word processors, and considerable laboratory testing facilities are all drawn in the vortex of the production of this machine. The consequences of its discontinuance would be disastrous and affect many thousands of jobs which directly and indirectly depend upon the initial political decision as to allocation of resources.

This is then the most attractive feature for the politician. It is his unique weapon in generating and directing surplus profit and influencing to some degree employment. Unlike the National Health Service or any other community orientated body, armaments are subject entirely to the whim and fancy of those who enjoy the ultimate political power. It is a whip and a carrot of immense effect and is eagerly justified. Yet the unfortunate truth remains. With very few exceptions those countries which have deliberately pursued the creation and recreation of an armoury of defensive weapons now have no political alternative to their retention as an essential element in their expenditure and investment programme. Each nation is preempted by its policy over some 40 years not in the sense that it cannot now admit to the absence of threat of real war, but that its economic policy depends on a large proportion of national income having to be directed towards the creation and construction of weapons of war.

Beveridge once said that it is better to pay men to dig holes in the road and then to fill them up rather than to pay them to do nothing. The logic is quite clear. The men remain fit, active and work practised. It may well be that the production of armaments that eventually rust away replace the holes and to that extent is economically justified. The regurgitation of a nation's wealth may have no useful or attractive product but at least it keeps certain muscles in trim in anticipation of future useful and rewarding work.

This remains a very weak justification for such a policy. Nevertheless, it is more than likely that the United Kingdom will continue to allocate a substantial proportion of its resources, changing its political posture only to the extent of moving from additional nuclear weapons towards so called conventional armaments. The latter are economically more attractive since decisions can be taken and changed with reasonable rapidity and the allocation is entirely within the U.K.'s discretion, that is that of British politicians.

It is highly probable, therefore, that in 1987/88 the British government will find a reason for relying upon the Americans entirely for nuclear weaponry and seek to obtain political mileage from a redirection of national investment entirely into conventional weapons.

Until 1945 the political justification for armaments was aggression or defence. War was a means of increasing or reforming economic resources and the investment in armaments was appropriate.

From 1945 to 1985 the political facade of fear of nuclear war enabled politicians to continue to allocate part of their respective nation's resources entirely at their discretion. Post 1985 the spectre of unemployment brought about primarily throughout techno-logical developments and the consequent possibility of social revolution will encourage politicians of every colour to continue to use the unfettered power given to them in the interests of national security. The nuclear armoury is already overflowing, so with grandiose courage the politician will take the risk of diverting his effort back into so-called conventional weapons.

Mention might also be made of the German economic strategy that is integrated with its policy on nuclear disarmament.

Since the early 1950's, West Germany's avowed intent has been reunification with its Eastern counterpart, an objective quietly and consistently supported by the populace of the latter. It has recognised that the main hurdle is the persuasion of the Russians. It also accepts the Russian fear of encirclement by its enemies. Its approach is therefore quite simple. At the appropriate time, it will endeavour to prove to the Russians that the substantial land mass represented by the combined Germanies and guaranteed to be neutral will forever provide an effective European defence against Western aggression. The other side of that argument to its European friends is that the combined Germanies will offer them the same defence and to remove any misunderstanding on that score will lay down its people as potential non-nuclear lambs for slaughter should the Russians renege. The offer is virtually worthless, since it is extremely unlikely that Russia would take a nuclear initiative in Europe. Nevertheless it has considerable political attraction and will undoubtedly be accepted.

Germany's economic strategy relies upon avoidance of signifi-cant expenditure upon arms that will never be used, control of its domestic market by ignored cartels, maintaining internal low prices (and incidentally the lowest possible internal rate of inflation) an export trade dependent upon service and quality and the control of marginal labour (known as foreign labour). All these elements are assisted by the present trade relationship with Eastern Germany and are also anticipatory of re-unification. For example, the Federal Republic enjoys the manufacture and marketing of products which bear internationally famous names but whose head offices are by the quirk of geographic division in the Democratic Republic. This pleasant condition is attained by licence agreements which are both legitimate and highly beneficial. Similarly, where price is more sensitive and a general image of reliability is required, mass produced goods are imported by Western Germany from Eastern Germany at advantageous prices which take into account the desirable attributes of the Deutschmark. These goods can then be trade marked by the importer and exported north, south or west. Whilst the present trading relationship is somewhat one-sided – there being no point in accelerating the growth of the Russian controlled economy which would only delay reunification – it provides a sound and expandable base for the new Germany.

The ethics and morality of this scenario are of no interest to the economist. It is the probable behaviour pattern of man and if it is confirmed then it is possible to forecast clearly and without ambiguity the most effective policies that can be designed to fit within the conditions that are anticipated.

It is unlikely that man will ever beat his sword into a plough. Indeed the reverse will be more likely. Politicians will suggest that he needs both, the one to protect himself and the other to better himself. In the production of the former he will learn how to facilitate the production of the latter. To that extent it will improve the job prospects for blacksmiths.

Drawing Threads Together

Economics is the study of the activity of man in his attempts to improve his physical lot. Man in this context is not the individual, but the mass.

Man's attitude and reactions never change. His pattern of behaviour is therefore constant and recurring. It can be forecast.

Motivation and incentive are as irrelevant as religion, philosophy and morals in the economic activity of man.

The ambition of man is power without responsibility. Power is applied to achieve security and comfort. Power is therefore abdicated to those who promise man security and comfort.

Amongst man there are individuals whose behaviour pattern as a class is also constant. They are those who find personal satisfaction in the use of power.

Amongst man is also a tiny minority who own resources that can provide long term support to those who seek to use power. It is this minority that can direct the achievement of man.

Man's struggle is within a given environment which responds only in part to his endeavours. Man has some discretion in the uses of his environment. His defence against the unknown is integrity of observation and analysis.

Those without resources who seek power are politicians. In pursuance of power they are obliged to represent and misrepresent. They can only achieve personal goals by division. Politicians appeal to the strongest emotions of man, fear, envy and greed to achieve the maximum reaction and the quickest response. Man is eager to hear promises and to abdicate responsibility. Power is given.

Resources that are helpful in the short term and essential in the long term for the attainment of the objectives of those to whom power has been given respond only to the motivation of fear, since retention of resources is the primary objective of their owners. Politicians who gain their support are assured of a greater continuity of office than those who depend exclusively on the popular vote.

All economic activities have a finite life cycle which can be pre-determined. Change is inevitable and must be pre-empted. Avoidance of change is temporary and disastrous. Planning is emasculated without implementation. Planning for decline is as important as planning for growth. Decisions must be matters of choice and not the acceptance of the inevitable.

Political decisions generate economic results which are usually the opposite of the intentions. Political intervention assumes motivations and imposes patterns of behaviour. Friction may assist but political intervention always diminishes economic achievement.

The improvement of the lot of man leads inevitably to a surplus of capacity to produce so that supply will always exceed demand. Surplus production is the manipulative key of the politician who uses fear to justify his exclusive responsibility for its consumption.

War in the form of aggression and destruction has been superseded by war in the form of economic domination. Nations that evolve international strategies and organise their industrial and commercial activities to accord with such strategies are more likely to succeed economically than those who have no such strategy or at best optimise their internal capabilities.

Economic warfare could be the ultimate solution to man's desire to enjoy the optimum use of the world's resources.

All economic activities are inter-related. No decision can be taken in isolation. To hope without the justification of experience is to court disaster. To assume that man will change as far as his economic activities are concerned is to accord him a capability that does not exist. To hope and to assume are the hallmarks of political intervention.

Economics is a study of integrity. It sees what has happened and therefore what is likely to happen. It does not cast judgement and accepts that which it studies may not of itself be honest, but then neither may be man. Economics may not like what it sees or the outcome of the application of its logic. Just as it ignores motivation as an area of speculation, economics accepts that as a study in observation it must itself be unemotional and unemotive. Those discolourations are best left to the politician.

Work has been promoted to a social ethic, necessary for the fulfilment of man, a regimented industry and an economic necessity. Work is politically presented as a right regardless of need or circumstance.

Wages are presented as a reward for work and are assumed to equal effort. The concept of work needs radical re-examination. Wages relate the measurement of recipient satisfaction to the creation of added value. Wages are paid in return for the offer of effort and ability. Work is provided by the employer.

Unemployment is the lack of wages other than in the form of government grant.

Nationalisation and Privatisation are the same product in different packages. The introduction of entrepreneurial thinking has expanded the opportunities for both.

The velocity of money is far more critical and sensitive than its volume in circulation. Its use as working capital determines the profitability of an investment. Currency is a commodity and a vehicle for speculation. Oil dominates currency to the advantage of the latter as it is now possible to isolate international currency fluctuations from national economies.

Inflation is the lack of balance between added value and its constituent parts of capital return and repayment and the cost of labour.

Political measurements of inflation are misleading and relatively meaningless. They serve a pre-conceived purpose. The economic measurement of inflation identifies the appropriate course of action necessary to alleviate excessive problems that might otherwise arise. Controlled inflation is a necessary and positive attribute in an economic society. Deflation can be more dangerous than uncontrolled inflation. "Galloping" inflation is an economic state which has characteristics and causes that set it quite apart even from the violent inflationary movements experienced during the trading development of a nation. It is a specific disease which requires a particular cure and is not an extension of a lesser complaint.

It is doubtful whether Trade Unions have significantly improved the lot of the worker if the effect of the Socialist Party and the economic facts of life are excluded. There is no doubt that in the future Trade Unions have to change their constitution and role in society if they are to make any worthwhile contribution. There is a significant opportunity for them in the political arena and from there to exert economic influence in the division of the wealth created by the nation.

Politicians have been economically hoist on the petard of armaments. They will not readily relinquish the weapon of control and influence — namely the unilateral disposition of a large proportion of a country's wealth.

The wealth of the United Kingdom is unique only in the pattern and combination of its resources and capabilities. Other countries have similar and sometimess better individual strengths, but none has the complete profile. That profile will and must change as environmental opportunities arise and disappear. The country's wealth is a kaleidoscope of resources the pattern of which is deliberately and pre-necessity changed in anticipation of the need thereby maximising its impact and use. The key resource of the United Kingdom is its people. Its main ingredient is its history. Its opportunities are infinite. Just as a man's grasp should be within his reach, the economic grasp of the United Kingdom is within the reach of its leadership.

A country that has an agreed economic philosophy knows where it is going. It can afford economic policies that might favour some sections of its community to the preference of others. It can even afford the costs of frustrated and vascillating economic policies.

Public acceptance of an economic philosophy can transform a politician into a statesman. A statesman is an effective leader because he acknowledges an ultimate reality for the nation as a whole and plans its achievement.

Economics is the study of man in the mass and concerns itself with his reaction when placed in a prescribed environment. Why he reacts as he does is irrelevant. In theory to know why is to provide an answer to all future problems. In practice, man cannot be analysed as if he were a macro-copy of an individual.

Machiavelli studied princes intensively. He knew what to expect of them, but he never aspired to understand them and they were a tiny and select band of men. The motivation of the peasants was not a study undertaken by Machiavelli. He knew only too well that that which they themselves did not comprehend could not possibly be understood by others. The objective of the few had to be power. As for the many, the prince of observers would have undoubtedly subscribed to the view that for them, "blessed are they that expect nothing, for they will surely not be disappointed."

Where Now?

Whatever the impact of social and technological revolutions, of war and peace, of famine and plenty, of natural and industrial disasters, man himself has not changed one jot since the life and times of Machiavelli. In this fact lies the hope for the future that however confusing or complex his environment, he will be able to maintain his balance and course as long as he continues to examine critically and honestly his circumstances and his probable behavourial reaction to them.

There has been one highly significant change since Machiavelli. Over the last two centuries, the politician has usurped the prince. The natural fickleness of power has been grossly exaggerated by the vulnerability of leadership dependent upon the popular vote. Politics and economics have been deliberately and unnecessarily fused. Man's baser emotions have been raised, tapped and manipulated in an eagerly promoted mad scramble for pieces of the promised national pancake. He has been deliberately discouraged from raising his standards, his thoughts and his eyes for fear that discovery of his place in the political universe will cause him to question and then to think. Far better for the purposes of the politician that man's standard of living should be transient satiation and preferential satisfaction.

Nevertheless, economics is still not a study of morals, social responsibility or religious concepts. It is confined to the ways in which man seeks to improve his lot, whatever his choice or persuasion.

Acceptance of current conditions as unavoidable is the hallmark of the lazy fool. The price of careless acquiescence far exceeds the cost of positive effort. The weakness of the politician ensures ultimate economic disaster. Unlike the prince, the politician seeks power as a means to an end — grandiosity.

In an alleged democracy, a politician lacks the certainty of being able to pass on his power to his future generations. He can only ensure that his family benefits whilst he is in power and then only indirectly. He therefore lacks time.

A politician assumes responsibility for one section of a community and deliberately leads it into battle against another section of the same community. He survives only as long as the battle rages. He therefore lacks national leadership.

A politician must uphold political dogma irrespective of logic and common sense. He is unable to sustain a long term philosophy. He therefore lacks credibility.

A politician measures his performance against that of his opponents and not the needs of his nation. He therefore lacks worthwhile standards.

The politician is indeed a pauper when compared with the prince of the past and those national economies that place their trust and future in his hands can expect even shorter shrift than that anticipated of the princes by Machiavelli.

. In 1986, the United Kingdom has no agreed economic philosophy or strategy. It does not even possess an agreed national economic policy. Without a philosophy it cannot offer its people any purposeful or satisfying challenge for the twenty-first century. It cannot expect a place in the sun despite past providence.

The absence of an agreed economic policy simply means that the national ship has no rudder. Since it already has neither course nor compass, the political pilot can happily justify the absence of any appendix to his wheel. He can merrily spin it either way with equal effect.

However valid the criticism it has no substance unless it can be translated into a positive alternative to that which it pulls to pieces. Observations on the past and present only have substance when they can be extended as recommendations for the future. If it is accepted in principle that the United Kingdom needs a long term economic philosophy designed to benefit the nation as a whole and to resist the overtures of international competitors, then if Machiavellian Economics has anything to offer it should at least set out how that might be achieved.

There would appear to be no more profitable or practical approach to the construction of a U.K. economic philosophy than that adopted by international corporations in undertaking the same task. Applying those principles, the stages involved would be as follows:-

1. A detailed analysis of U.K. strengths, resources, capabilities and capacities as to people, industry, commerce and physical resources.

2. A construction of the U.K. economic profile as it is and will be in the immediate future.

3. An analysis of international competitors differentiating between those that are directly comparable and competitive (e.g. Germany, France and Italy) those that are comparable and indirectly competitive (e.g. O.P.E.C. and certain developing countries), those that are directly competitive but incomparable (e.g. U.S.A. and Japan) those that are indirectly competitive and incomparable (e.g. Russia and China), such other classifications as may be appropriate together with the identification of their respective policies, strengths, resources, etc.

4. An analysis and projection of global technological developments and opportunities.

5. Preliminary attempts at defining practical and acceptable U.K. international economic philosophies with consideration of their implications and benefits.

6. Identification of a specific philosophy that accords with opportunities and capabilities.

7. Consideration of internal implications of the preferred international economic philosophy on national policies related to such matters as taxation, employment, living standards etc. etc.

8. Consideration of impact of national policies on political dogma (ways and means of sharing the national cake).

The amount of work involved is enormous but well within the academic resources of the United Kingdom. To put the load into perspective, it would be more than reasonable to state that no chairman of an international corporation would attempt to lead his company with less information and understanding.

Although there is an inevitable similarity between the steps necessary to construct an international economic philosophy for a country and an international business strategy for a corporation, there are significant differences between the respective results. There are many aspects of a given ultimate reality for a nation that set it apart from the objectives of a corporation, however large or powerful the latter may be.

Those who accept responsibility for the leadership of a people undertake a task that they know they cannot finish. The objective of a nation must be so many years ahead that even the probability of its attainment is itself remote. The time scale of an international economic philosophy is geometric, whilst that for a corporation is, in relative terms, arithmetic.

Probably the most critical difference, however, is to be found in the methods open to each set of "managers" in order to get things done. The statesman depends upon persuasion. He is obliged to accept responsibility for the effects of his decisions even though the cause and effect are imagined. He cannot coerce except for very short periods of time and he is heavily dependent upon those who believe that they do not depend upon him.

Finally, there is the continuous resistance against change. In a corporation, since the ultimate sanction is command, overt resistance can be swiftly overcome. In a community, the necessity for an order is quickly denounced as the final failure.

Despite these fundamental differences, the analogy between corporation and nation remains apposite since it assumes a self-imposed discipline of getting to know the total current environment, its implications and opportunities, and thereafter consistently extrapolating its probable evolution. Unlike the present political perambulations, economic philosophy starts with a broad canvas and leaves the recognition of the signature to others.

The first requisite of man is to know himself. The second is to know where he is. The third is to decide where he can and will go. Then, but only then, can he expect to achieve the personal satisfaction of a successful completed journey. Thus it is with Machiavellian Economics.